WHAT IS THE SHARIA?

What is the Sharia?

BAUDOUIN DUPRET

THE AGA KHAN UNIVERSITY
(International) in the United Kingdom

Institute for the Study of Muslim Civilisations

Published in Association with the Aga Khan
University Institute for the Study of Muslim
Civilisations (AKU-ISMC)

HURST & COMPANY, LONDON

First published in French as La Charia: Des sources à la pratique, un concept pluriel by Éditions La Découverte in 2014.

First published in the United Kingdom in 2018 by
C. Hurst & Co. (Publishers) Ltd.,
41 Great Russell Street, London, WC1B 3PL
© Baudouin Dupret, 2018
Translation © David Bond
Printed in India
The right of Baudouin Dupret to be identified as the author
of this publication is asserted by him in accordance with the
Copyright, Designs and Patents Act, 1988.

Distributed in the United States, Canada and Latin America by
Oxford University Press, 198 Madison Avenue, New York,
NY 10016, United States of America.

A Cataloguing-in-Publication data record for this book
is available from the British Library.

ISBN: 9781849048170

www.hurstpublishers.com

The opinions expressed in this volume are those of the authors
and do not necessarily reflect those of the Aga Khan University
Institute for the Study of Muslim Civilisations.

Contents

A Note on Quotations

This book contains quotations from works written and published in French. For the convenience of readers, these appear in English.

Introduction

'Today in Morocco the Sharia[1] means countering immorality and corruption, finding work for people, and educating citizens. The Sharia as *hudud* has not existed for a long time in the nation.' This observation is interesting for a number of reasons. It is a quotation from a statement by the first Islamist politician to head a Moroccan government, after the victory of his party, the Moroccan Justice and Development Party, in the legislative elections of November 2011. First, the statement shows us how the Sharia imposes itself as a recurrent theme in public debate. It also shows us that this theme is more about the interpretation of a dogma than about an evident and intangible truth. It underlines the ethical rather than legal dimension of the reference to the Sharia, while highlighting its intrinsically political nature. In addition, the statement indicates how the Sharia is historically grounded, and that it is therefore a contingent and malleable concept, one capable of evolution. Lastly, it shows us that the Sharia is characterized more easily by what it is not, or is no longer, than by its substance. This study seeks to clarify this tangle of words, understandings, positions, preconceived ideas, and scholarly considerations. At the same time, clarification does not mean declaring what is just and what is true, and distinguishing truth from error. Rather, it means drawing up a 'map' which enables us to navigate and avoid as far as possible obstacles and intellectual dead-ends, as well as hasty approaches which can prevent us from appreciating the topography of the terrain we are studying, its constituent detail, and its inherent richness.

An object of polemic with contrasting uses

'Western imagination has constructed a dramatic hostility to Islam.'[2] This is probably derived from the successive stages of Western discovery of the East from the Crusades to colonialism, up to the twenty-first century. The West issues – pell-mell – denunciations of terrorism, military regimes, tyranny, fundamentalism, authoritarianism, the hegemony of religion, and intolerance. Islam is discussed only in the context of events associated with conflict, as though its only function was to serve as a foil. Islam, it seems, characterizes everything emanating from distant non-Western latitudes, as if it was unable to lead a life of peaceful routine far removed from warlike fury. Because there is a refusal to seriously engage with those realities of which the reference to Islam is the expression, and because Islam is manipulated for political reasons which take little account of the people and the communities concerned, this religion and its associated norms have become a repository of imaginings which generate anxiety. It is not possible to have a static view of the Islamic world as eternally stuck in the Middle Ages. This very idea of a Dark Age across which a bridge is built in order to link two Golden Ages is used in Europe to found the 'narcissistic history of its modernity'.[3]

In these procedures of stigmatization, words play a preponderant role. They give an appearance of objectivity, which seems to correspond to a reality, while actually suggesting more than they describe. Such words, as they stand, are far removed from the understanding of the general public. A certain erudition is required to know what terms such as *fiqh*, *qadi*, *halal*, *imam*, or *jihad* can mean. At the same time these words resonate, and are associated with connotations rather than exact descriptions. Nebulous references, vague ideas, and prejudices surround these words, giving them a meaning, but one that is remote from their technical or scholarly definitions. This is particularly true of what concerns Islam and the Sharia in relation to which Western societies cultivate a 'Lepanto complex'. 'The world of Islam is not always in the foreground, but is present in the background and seen overall as the ideological adversary of Christian society which, in its entirety, is in conflict with Islam.'[4] One should be circumspect with regard to words imported from Arabic in so far as the lack of translation corresponds to a large extent with a desire to identify by connotation and, thereby, to disqualify. The preference of some terms over others, such as Allah to God or jihad to holy war, is not innocent. What one might think of as synonyms in fact generate multiple meanings which mark a particular form of discourse and its unstated objectives. The words chosen by an Arabic speaker transmit a particular value which is derived from the context in which it is used. The use of Arabic terms by a foreign non-Arabic speaker adds to the connotations associated with these words, in a broadly pejorative way. The effect is frequently to reinforce dichotomies between fellow citizens and foreigners, between a model and its opposite, namely the West and its East.

Islam and the Sharia are, above all, points of reference in countries and societies the majority of whose populations are Muslim. It would be an error to think that perceptions are unanimous, homogeneous, and monolithic. In Islamic settings, as elsewhere, Islam and Sharia are words and concepts whose meaning and significance vary in space and time. One cannot claim that there is one way of reading the Quran or the Prophetic Tradition from which the Sharia, the Islamic norm, emerges. One must recognize that even for the most dogmatic believers and scholars, revelation has given rise to varied readings and interpretations. Each of them makes claims to truth, often to the exclusion of other, rival claims, but that does not prevent one from perceiving the plural nature of Muslim religiosity – although pluralism would be an overstatement.

The question of the Sharia is raised so vigorously today because we live at a time when the vocabulary of Islam constitutes a major resource in the social, political, and ethical reconfigurations of the various Islamic worlds. The use of this discursive register and Islamic lexicon should be understood in the context of colonization, independence, the formation of new states, migration, and globalization, as well as modernity and postmodernity. This return to Islam can assume pietistic forms, with an increase in the observation of religious obligations and rituals, or quietist forms, when calls for indifference to politics are made. Islam and its Law, the Sharia, have been mobilized for political ends by numerous states, movements, and individuals. This is what has generally been termed 'Islamism' – an ambiguous term given that it meant, in the recent past, belonging to the Muslim confession. Islamism has come to entail a double affirmation: in a positive sense, a return to Islamic precepts seen as containing the solution to all the evils of our time; and, in a negative sense, the rejection of Western domination, of whatever ideological stripe. Islamism is therefore a political project which uses the heritage of the West as a foil, while legitimizing the reappropriation of a number of its tenets.

There is, however, not one Islamist East but a multitude of tendencies, each of which, in its own way, seeks to bring 'Islamic' solutions to difficulties encountered by Muslims, as Muslims, on a daily basis. This tendency was accentuated when in 2011 several authoritarian regimes were shaken to their foundations and Islamic movements won successive electoral victories. These successes are unsurprising if one recalls that by the 1970s, at the very least, political contestation had basically moved away from the left towards a rhetoric of authenticity. In cultural terms, the message of authenticity was more readily acceptable and was all the more effective given that its proponents were excluded from government. 'Authenticity' capitalized on the repressive and authoritarian tendencies of existing regimes. However, it would be false to believe that Islamism was a monopoly of opposition movements, given the extent to which Islamic rhetoric had imposed itself in both public and private space. In other words, the opposing camps were divided not by fundamental ideological differences but by questions relating to the exercise of power and challenges to it.

The contemporary context is one in which multiple sources of reference are used simultaneously. These include Islam, democracy, and law. Numerous political concepts that originate outside the Islamic world are used within this context. One can affirm that these concepts have been progressively 'naturalized' and that they have come to form part of the vocabulary of the immense majority of the actors on the political stage in this Islamic world. There may on occasion be challenges to this vocabulary, but they remain marginal, and above all are rhetorical packaging rather than original conceptual research. They reflect a desire to re-establish historical continuity rather than to make a decisive break between past and present. This is the case in the field of norms, including legal norms. One cannot perceive a distinct frontier between the proponents of the Sharia, on the one hand, and the rule of law, on the other. Few if any movements call for the exclusion of a reference to Islam and Islamic normativity in the name of the principle of separation between state and religion. There is, however, a wide spectrum of views between those who claim that the prevailing legal and constitutional system is illegitimate and those who accept it without major difficulties, between those who accept the right of religious minorities to assume public office and those who reject it, and between proponents of the equality of religions and those who assign religions a place in a hierarchy of precedence.

The Sharia in a few words

Shariʿa is, first, an Arabic word which does not have its own clear, obvious, and universal meaning. Only the term's uses across space and time can convey to us what Sharia is. In other words, the term does not have an intrinsic meaning accessible to, at any rate, human understanding. To grasp the meaning of Sharia, context must be taken into account. Is it the perspective of the nascent Shafiʿi school in ninth-century Baghdad, or that of Jalal al-Din Rumi in thirteenth-century Konya? The Ottoman Empire in the Tanzimat period in the nineteenth century or the Egyptian Muslim

Brotherhood in the twentieth century? Is it a question of doctrinal production, judicial practice, or political demands? The term derives its meaning only from the ways in which it is used. What is said and understood of the Sharia can therefore only be understood in the present context, and not in ethereal, weightless terms. When one begins to study Sharia as a term, it should be discussed as a language game. One notices that the term can sometimes assume a legal sense, as in the case of 'Islamic law', sometimes a political sense, when in an election campaign there are calls for 'the application of Sharia'. Putting these language games in perspective allows us to see the extent to which the term can function as a rallying point for identity: on the one hand, it is used to promote a specific heritage; on the other, it serves as a bogey.

The traditional viewpoint has been that the Quran and the Tradition of the Prophet (the narration of his acts and words) are the two pillars of Islamic law. One should note that the Quranic text, as it took definitive form in the fifty years after the death of Muhammad, and the corpus of the Sunna (the Tradition), as it accumulated over two centuries from the time of the Hegira, the beginning of the Islamic era, are only marginally concerned by prescription and proscription, what is recommended and what is forbidden. The sacred book and the Tradition are above all composed of elements of mystical inspiration, moral exhortations, and edifying stories. They reflect the context of the revelation of the Quran to Muhammad, the Arabia of the sixth and seventh centuries, and the life of the Prophet, who transformed himself from preacher to head of an incipient religious community. In addition, these two main sources of the Sharia, in the course of their constitution as well as in their final form, have always depended on the readings proposed by their respective specialists. One can think here in particular of the important tendencies within Islam represented by Shi'ism and Sunnism and the four main Sunni schools (*madhahib*): Maliki, Hanafi, Shafi'i, and Hanbali.

References to the Sharia are not frequent in the Quran. In reality, most classical scholars did not evoke the Sharia and did not claim to know it, because this would have meant declaring oneself equal to God, thus committing the capital sin of associationism. Writings on Islamic normativity, from the ninth century onward, assumed the features of a particular form known as *fiqh*. The best translation one can give of this term is 'doctrine'. Treatises were produced in each of the great Sunni schools as in the wider Shi'a family, followed by commentaries and summaries. In parallel, the technique of consultation to obtain a legal opinion (*fatwa*) became widespread, and collections and compilations of such consultations were often made. One should underline the effect of the emergence of empires, notably the Ottoman Empire, on Islamic normativity, when one of the schools became official state doctrine. As a result of colonization or the pressure exerted by European powers, numerous countries embarked on a process of reform which led in most cases to the transformation of Islamic normativity into an Islamic code of legislation.

Knowledge of Islamic normativity – that is to say, its doctrine – is one of the main disciplines of scholarly Islam. A science of the foundations of the knowledge of this normativity (*'ilm usul al-fiqh*) was developed in order to set out its sources clearly and rationalize its methodology. According to modalities which can vary from one school to another, this science has four foundations: the Holy Book (Quran), the Prophetic Tradition (Sunna), consensus among Muslims and their scholars (*ijma'*), and analogical reasoning (*qiyas*). The great scholar Muhammad al Shafi'i (d. 820) is the leading scholar in the science of the foundations of doctrine. Among other things, he enabled the relationship between the first two sources, the Quranic text and the Prophetic Traditions, to be clarified.

Treatises of *fiqh* are always concerned in the first place with ritual obligations associated with Islamic devotion. These are the five pillars of Islam: the profession of faith (*shahada*); ritual prayer (*salat*); almsgiving (*zakat*); fasting (*sawm*); and pilgrimage (*hajj*). To this are often added requirements of ritual purity and dietary interdictions. Second, these treatises are concerned especially with family relations, an area on which Islamic rules concentrate: marriage, divorce, filiation, succession. It is among these family-related rules that one finds numerous prescriptions and proscriptions which are the object of debate today, such as the rights of guardianship over women, the endowment of wives by their husbands, the authority of husbands and their unilateral right to dissolve a marriage, the imbalance in the duties of wives and husbands, and unequal inheritance rights determined by gender. One should note that the exercise of justice, in the context of medieval and modern Islamic societies, was generally separate from the activity of doctrinal production. On the basis of his knowledge of *fiqh* a judge had a wide margin of discretion. Often he based his decision on the results of consultation with an expert, the *mufti*.

What is called 'Islamic law' does not correspond to a reality as ancient as Islam itself. The idea of transforming norms into law and, in particular, into codified law is the result of an invention rooted in the European intrusion on to the Islamic scene. Orientalist scholars and colonial administrators, on the one hand, and Muslim rulers and new elites, on the other, sought in *fiqh* material susceptible of being poured into the mould of a Napoleonic-style law code. This grafting process was successful, and today the notion of Islamic law is an element of the ordinary and normal horizons of political and juridical thought in Muslim-majority societies as well as societies with strong Muslim minorities. Islamic law therefore was codified, especially in the area of family relations with which *fiqh* was particularly concerned. The term 'personal status law' is used to describe this legislation. Most countries with a majority-Muslim population have a specific family code which in general, in a highly variable measure, is inspired by the precepts of the normativity. *Fiqh* continues to exercise an influence in another area, that of the pious foundations (*waqf*s). One can also discern religious inspiration in other domains, such as finance. Most often it is a question of contemporary developments on subjects that have only been sketchily treated by *fiqh* but for which a disposition can be found in the sacred text which can provide a justification for their regulation. This includes, for example, the Quranic prohibition of usury. A relatively recent phenomenon can be observed with regard to the constitutions of Muslim-majority states, namely the referencing of the Sharia as a source of legislation. It is no longer a case here of codifying Islamic normativity but of directing the attention of contemporary legislators to this normativity so that it can inspire their research.

The Sharia has also become a political slogan. It is not so much a case of converting the Sharia into Islamic law as of staking a claim to the Sharia in the face of regimes whose credibility, including their religious authenticity, is contested. Most of the time, political parties calling for the application of the Sharia do not have a programme detailing its content, and what should be abrogated and replaced in existing juridical systems. Application of the Sharia is above all a claim of political ethics and the marking out of a reference rather than the implementation of a precise programme.

The presence of Muslims in countries where they do not form a majority has led to the emergence of numerous questions. Some are legal in nature and concern the recognition of rights inspired by Islamic law in states that are overwhelmingly secular. Others concern the practice of religion and the possibility of living out one's faith in societies where the predominant reference points are human rights and the principle of the religious neutrality of the state. The question of Islamic normativity is not a legal one, but is ethical and deontological – that is to say, moral. The question is how to live in conformity with one's convictions in societies whose populations may for the most part not share these convictions.

The Sharia is indeed Islamic Law, a Law with a capital L, as it is of divine origin. To make it distinct from man-made law we speak of Islamic norm or normativity. Like all revealed religions Islam includes rules, a series of prescriptions and prohibitions. This affirmation does not, however, take us very far. It remains for us to determine the sources from which this normativity derives, their order of precedence, how the norm has been interpreted, how scholars and believers have appropriated it, and, above all, what forms the normativity might assume in the twenty-first century. There are two possible perspectives for the observer whose approach is not inspired by dogma: first, a presentation of the different understandings of the term Sharia through history; and second, a discussion of its present-day signification. This book takes up the challenge of this twofold exercise.

1

A Concept and Its Contexts

The term Sharia (*shari'a*) possesses for the believer an intrinsic meaning which it is not our intention either to reject or to adopt. The sole tenable position consists of observing what is said about the Sharia and give an account of this, indicating in what circumstances and how it is used. In this respect we must recognize the multiple understandings of the term – through time and space, but also from one person to another, and, even more, from one context to another. If we set aside any act of faith while engaged in our descriptive task, the Sharia becomes a concept which is accessible to the understanding only if one studies its practical manifestations, while leaving aside the question of whether such a manifestation corresponds truly to the 'true' or 'false', 'orthodox' or 'heterodox' meaning of the word.

Two examples can help to gauge the variety of understandings of the term. The first is a personal anecdote. In 1992 in Cairo, having had various personal possessions stolen in my home, I took the case to the police. The police pursued their investigations, and the thief and his accomplice were caught. I was summoned to the central police station in Cairo, and declared that I had identified the thief after the suspect was shown to me. He asked me to intercede in his favour with the police authorities. Once back in the police inspector's office I said that I did not want to drop the case, while specifying that I did not seek vengeance. At that point the inspector replied directly to me: 'If we were in an Islamic state and the Sharia was applied, he should have his hand cut off. He is lucky that our civil law is less strict than the religious Law.'[1]

A different place, other customs, another example: in Britain a storm of protest was caused in 2008 by a suggestion from the Archbishop of Canterbury that some form of recognition be given to the Sharia in the country's legal system. Radical commentators seized the chance to prophesy that the 'banner of the Sharia' would one day float over Downing Street. Their claims were based on an imaginary figure of 500 conversions each day, which would give the country a Muslim majority by 2020. At the opposite end of the spectrum, one of the organizers of a large demonstration in London around the slogan 'One law for all, no Sharia' declared that 'religions are often sources of oppression, but the Sharia is particularly oppressive.'[2]

However, as indicated in the introduction to this work, the Sharia was held to be largely unknowable by most of the thinkers of the classical period: Sharia referred to divine normativity, and claiming to know this was as good as taking oneself for the equivalent of God. Most scholars preferred to speak of their 'opinion' in this regard. On the other hand, since the mid-twentieth century anyone can claim to know what the word signifies and how it must be applied. That does not mean that there is general agreement on this signification and how it should be put into practice. Great confusion surrounds the subject of Sharia: customs linked to countries and societies of origin of immigrant populations; rules deduced from a corpus of canonical texts; law in Muslim-majority countries; the political legitimacy of a regime; rules of personal and collective ethics; and many other elements.

The Sharia in language games

It is not certain that questions such as 'What is religion?' or 'What is law?' can be answered. We are not dealing with things in themselves, but with uses of words some (not to say many) of which have a normative signification and are closely related to concepts derived from languages, cultures, institutions, and different contexts and activities. Words and concepts have in common not so much definitions as analogous usages, which one might describe as 'grammar'. Religion and law do not belong to a physical world whose terms correspond to external realities. They belong to the conceptual world, and as such acquire their meaning in the

17

context of their use. This is true of the term 'Islamic law' as well as 'Sharia'.

There is also a danger in talking of 'law' when one is dealing with different types of norm: things generally considered as totally different can be seen as similar; a specific historical concept can be used as a sociological instrument; a function of social control can be attributed to phenomena that do not necessarily possess this quality. Every attempt to define the concept of Islamic law creates rather than resolves an enigma, often by associating or excluding elements considered intrinsic or external to law. Such attempts at definition also lack awareness of the contextual and situated comprehension of the term, its derivatives and equivalents, as well as the fact that one term is not used exclusively to describe one thing, but can evoke very different concepts, depending on the situation.

Let us take another example. In treatises of Islamic doctrine or *fiqh*, chapters on ritual ablutions preceding the act of prayer constitute an important and recurrent element. As the tendency is to say 'Sharia' when one sees the term *fiqh* and 'Islamic law' when one hears the term 'Sharia', all the dispositions relating to these ablutions are often characterized as 'legal'. It is, however, difficult to perceive these as law, at least according to contemporary understandings of the term. The confusion is therefore complete.

One can also observe how the corpus of Islamic norms has tended to be characterized as 'law' at a particular historical moment. While it is a commonplace to say that the expression 'Islamic law' is a category of language, this should nevertheless be repeated so that the consequences of this affirmation are no longer a source of futile objections. A linguistic term is the product of a history and context, and in the case of Islamic law is the result of a specific project of understanding, control, and reframing of rules and usages which operated in the various environments where Islam was implanted. It is Orientalist science that conferred on them, from the nineteenth century, the characteristics of law, as that science understood this term. Discussion of 'Islamic law' in the nineteenth century means discussion of a historically situated concept which in a certain sense has assumed the characteristics of something natural. It remains to be seen what is covered by this somewhat 'bucket' concept.

The grammar – that is to say, the ordering of terms such as 'Islamic law' and 'Sharia' – must be examined in its contexts of use. Words do not possess an essential meaning accessible only in their language of origin. Their meaning is derived from the circumstances of their use. In different circumstances Islamic law and Sharia can be a reference to Islam in a legal context; a slogan denouncing the illegitimacy of a political regime; a concept identified with Islamic normativity before the nineteenth century; a symbol of the backwardness of Islamic societies; or a term of constitutional vocabulary. This range of meanings shows that these words do not have a substantial definition. The analysis of the ways the words are used allows three thorny questions to be clarified: how a single word can have different meanings; how different words can share features which give them a related signification; and how the heterogeneous nature of languages in no way prevents conceptual similarity between certain of their terms.

When the term 'Islamic law' is used to describe Islamic normativity or to translate the term 'Sharia', a category mistake is made which consists of describing one phenomenon with words used to describe another, different phenomenon. 'Islamic law' is a term that emerged in the wake of the imposition of legal systems founded on a formalist and rationalist bureaucratic model. The same holds true for jurisprudential doctrine, the theory of the foundations of doctrine, the practice of tribunals in a given period, and the technique of jurisprudential consultation: all of these can be described as long as one remains closely aware of the historical, social, and geographical character of all these phenomena.

Beyond dogmatic discourse, observation of practice

One can state with certitude that *shariʿa* is an Arabic word which means or alludes to divine teaching. It is therefore the divine Normativity. It is a normative concept on which across time and space a variety of contrasting meanings have been conferred. In this sense it is a form, a register, the inheritor today of previous practices and a matrix for the new practices of tomorrow. Rather than claiming that the Sharia is something, one can try to demonstrate what one makes it be. The most frequent attitude towards Sharia is what one could call 'essentialist'. This is the case in numerous scientific works which give the term Sharia a precise signification which, it is claimed, is the source that inspires the behaviour of millions of people. In one such work it is said, for example, that Islamic law (the usual equivalent for the terms Sharia and *fiqh*) continues to govern daily behaviour.[3] In the area of sexuality the author seems to suggest that the dispositions one can find in the treatises of *fiqh* continue to exercise an influence on commonly held perceptions and on contemporary juridical conceptions. Sexual relations that go beyond flirting, if not validated by a religious contract, are, it is claimed, categorized as forbidden, or *haram*. This demonstrates, for this author, that Muslim opinion persists in placing sexuality within the framework of religious law. However, it is difficult to prove such an affirmation, and when one looks more closely it could equally be a question of convenience, habit, conviction, or conformism. Nothing allows us to come to the conclusion that Islamic rules have been socially incorporated. On the contrary, it is probably the case that social rules were doctrinally appropriated.

In an even more emphatic way, it is claimed in another work that religion constitutes an entity that transcends historical, sociological, political, and cultural practice and conditioning, and that it forms a system independent of societies and their members.[4] Leaving practice aside, the author claims that religion occupies a central position across Islamic regions as it 'instils its categories and its representations in the hearts of the faithful ... it moulds their ways of thinking, confers upon them an attitude of mind, and tends to homogenize and render uniform discourse and behaviour'.[5] Religion therefore has an exceptional status in the same way as Sharia, the Law derived from religion. This, it is claimed, is a 'non-empirical' object, a mould which standardizes Muslim behaviour. The Law pre-exists individuals who refer to it, as if the religious system was not from beginning to end a practical fact: an enunciation of the rule, and its application, invocation, transgression, utilization, manipulation, ignorance, and so on.

This conception of things, which assumes that Muslims are genetically determined in their relationship to Sharia, is unsurprising when it emanates from a dogmatic discourse of, for example, scholars of Islam (the *'ulama*). It is untenable, however, in the universe of human and social science, which cannot accept historical and religious determinism, and, therefore, the idea that human beings are conditioned by their religious Law. Theories of incorporation make Muslims the instruments of this Law, whereas a practiced-based approach should maintain that the authority and the influence of the Sharia should be understood in context, studying who and what was involved, and in what circumstances. Rules and conduct cannot be dealt with separately. Sharia regulation is not as these authors depict it: it is not independent of practice, nor does it possess a predetermined clear sense. It also does not determine behaviour in a univocal way. Religious norms, like other norms, are a practical construction, and their authority derives from the power that humans attribute to them.

The academic conception of Sharia

The term 'Sharia' has been the object of many investigations which seek to delineate its meaning. These studies, through a particular methodology and within a particular discipline, seek to define what the word Sharia is and to what it refers, setting out what the word denotes. For the most part they concern its etymological, dogmatic, and historical meaning.

Let us take the example of Wael Hallaq's *Sharia: Theory, Practice, Transformations*.[6] In this work, the Sharia is treated as something particular, a specific and unique being whose ontogenesis and ontology one can study. It is an 'entity', belonging to a 'genus' which is 'designed to organize society and resolve disputes that threaten to disrupt [its order]'. It is, in addition, a 'lawgiver'. As such the Sharia is, it appears, 'incompatible' with other entities such as the state, 'a particular modern creature that fulfils fairly well-defined functions of governance and dominance'.[7] Of course, things become more complex and contradictory when one looks closer. If one accepts the point of view of the author, it is in the light of 'historical experience' that Islamic law is reluctant to accept political intervention, which means, ironically, that Sharia, while a timeless entity, only assumes an existence in the light of historical circumstances. In addition, the Sharia and the state, although belonging to the same genus, belong seemingly to different orders, which leads to the self-contradictory conclusion that they are incompatible because of their similar nature, despite their essential differences. 'In theory as well as in practice, both systems claim the ultimate legal sovereignty'[8] even if it is only in theory that Sharia considers the state as subject to its law, which means, in effect, that what is claimed to be true in theory and in practice is actually only true in theory. In addition, the Sharia is centrifugal in a horizontal sense whereas the state is vertically centripetal, despite historical experience in the Ottoman Empire where the organization of law was hierarchical, which implies that the Sharia is so well defined in theory that historical moments that do not fit with this theory are mere deviant exceptions. Sharia, it is claimed, is ideologically neutral and 'did not develop the need to hide itself behind an impenetrable ideology',[9] which would perhaps explain the failure of Islam to develop a modern economy and society, while the state is an 'ideological constitution the function of which is to misrepresent political and economic domination in ways that legitimate subjection'.[10] Finally, Sharia never aimed to exercise a monopoly over legitimate violence and to subordinate the state and the citizen to its systematic control, while the nation-state is the 'only entity in human history that has arrogated to itself this exclusive right'.[11] The ambition – common to Sharia and the state – to organize society and settle disputes produces, in the case of Sharia, a pluralist project and, in the case of the state, a hegemonic project.

It is superfluous to highlight the strange nature of this caricature of the modern state and, implicitly, of the law that derives from it. What is interesting is that it is a paradigmatic example of the conception that the scientific world can develop of the Sharia: it is seen as a timeless entity whose essential structures enable it to escape the disciplinary project of the modern nation-state. However, neither state nor Sharia possesses intentions, desires, a will, or objectives. They are constructions that constitute social reality, institutions created and inhabited by people for purposes as varied as the occasions on which they can attain these purposes. To attribute to state and Sharia intrinsic qualities and defects is as absurd as to attribute physical characteristics to God. A conceptual object exists only within the language games that relate to it.

There is a 'cultural lock' in the study of Sharia. This is due to a double attitude: on the one hand, there are inaccurate extrapolations based on specific knowledge – that is to say, a tendency to assume that knowledge of an aspect of Islamic culture allows one to comment in general on everything Islamic. Those competent in medieval Islamic theology are consulted, for example, in order to advance explanations of contemporary Islamic political radicalism. Claims are also made that a style of political thought rooted in the writings of classical authors, that of 'the power of obedience', has perpetuated itself. There is an attitude of omniscience with regard to the present day based on particularisms of culture and history. Such an attitude is an aporia because it implies that elements of languages and cultures are impermeable to translation. Thus it would be improper to speak of 'state' in an Islamic setting because this term, whose etymology refers to the idea of institution and stability, does not reflect the intrinsically unstable nature of power in Islam, reflected in the word *dawla*, whose etymology refers to the idea of cycles and instability.[12] Thus, again, authoritarianism is purportedly inherent to the Arab context which can only reproduce the 'same traditional schema' that imposes 'the figure of the despot', be it the Prophet in the writings of the famous Muslim scholar Ibn Khaldun in the fourteenth century or the philosopher as described by al-Farabi (*c.* 870–950) in the earlier medieval period.[13]

All these explanations, whether etymological, dogmatic, or historical, impose a similar conception on us, one simultaneously learned and simplistic, of what Sharia is and, above all, of what it does to people. Sometimes the discourse is apologetic, sometimes critical, or even derogatory. However, the question must not be approached in this way if we recognize, as Muslim specialists in jurisprudence did, that the designs of God are not accessible to human understanding, and that in consequence we can only describe what humans would have made of a word, were it divine.

A term with many connotations

The term Sharia is polysemous. It is an amalgam which captures the imagination of journalists and politicians as well as researchers and leads them to confuse 'law founded on the Qur'an and the Prophetic tradition, the norms of *fiqh*, the codified law of Muslim states, and the customary law of Muslim communities … from which there results a form of certitude about the content of Sharia, which in turn raises simple norms to a divine status with the aim of countering what is seen as the secular (and therefore human) form of other dispositions'.[14] While it is difficult to know what the term Sharia means precisely, one realizes that it is accompanied by affective, moral, and normative associations, both positive and negative.

The upheavals affecting numerous Arab countries from 2011 have put the question of the Sharia back on the agenda. Whether in Libya, Egypt or Tunisia, to mention only three countries, Sharia has been invoked by some and used as a bogey by others. In all these situations a common feature emerges: the term is seen as self-evident and its meaning is never questioned. Because of this, it is used as a resource for the construction of discourses of Islamophilia or Islamophobia, apologetics or denunciations, authenticity or alienation. In fact, 'Sharia' ends up connoting many things while denoting none. It is also true of a multitude of terms imported from a foreign language or loosely translated, and which have sometimes entered the dictionary: *fatwa*, *qadi*, *mullah*, *mufti*, *'ulama*, *imam*, *jihad*, *ayatollah*, and so on. Whether in the language of origin or in translation, there are words that say 'more than' or 'something else' distinct from the definition that the dictionary gives them. They transport modes of thought that, often, function in order to repeat certain representations of the world. The connotative effect of words of the Sharia is not limited to its Western usages – far from it. One should emphasize that the Sharia has become an ideological term before being legal, religious, ethical, or deontological. Sharia marks out the political space, demarcates the factions that struggle for the exercise of power, polarizes societies and the ways that they identify themselves in the eyes of the rest of the world. This is not based on content but on a mechanism of reference which imposes itself. Beyond the processes of glorification and diabolizing, the content of the reference is evanescent. It is alternately the ideal character of the city governed by Islam or the symbol of its backwardness that is highlighted.

Often, therefore, the divine normativity is defined less by a stable content than as the reflection of a political attitude and a way of being which consists of saying and doing like others in certain domains. Referring to the Sharia is therefore a way of taking a position or a type of conformism, one all the more solid because it refers to the divine prescription, which it is difficult to criticize lightly. Reference to the Sharia divides the world in two, between the 'respectable' and the 'others'. This is a politically productive distinction, 'since it contributes to legitimize or delegitimize actors'.[15] In addition, in an Islamic context, the Sharia enjoys credibility and wide acceptance, and not for merely political reasons: it is part of everyday life. What one understands by the term Sharia certainly varies from one person to another, from one corner of the world to another; but it is nevertheless true that in Islamic settings at least, the Sharia is a respectable reference that anyone can appropriate. Using the Sharia in politics is therefore natural and effective.

2

Exploring the Sources of the Divine Law
The Quran

In Arabic the word *shari'a* refers to the idea of a way, road, or access. It signifies a 'path of access to knowledge' or, in other terms, 'divine teaching', 'Law', or 'Norm' of God. The term is used for all the revealed Laws, whether Jewish, Christian, or Islamic. Classical sources – before the nineteenth century – make few references to Sharia. It is reputedly unknowable; the commentaries of scholars on Sharia belong to the field of doctrine (*fiqh*) which is the speciality of jurisconsults.

Fiqh, as its specialists recognize, is a human construction. One can reconstitute the history of its appearance and development, the debates and conflicts that it provoked, and the transformations it underwent. As this knowledge took form, the question was eventually raised of the appropriate methodology for distinguishing its sources, putting them in order, and determining the relation between them. This is the science of the foundations of the knowledge of doctrine (*'ilm usul al-fiqh*).

In order to begin to discuss the Sharia, one must also discuss the sources of its science as identified by Muslim scholars, the *'ulama*, and the four principal foundations which Sharia recognized: the Holy Book or Quran; Prophetic Tradition; the consensus (*ijma'*) of Muslims or their scholars; and analogical reasoning (*qiyas*) and its variants. Let us survey these four sources, setting out the historical and social conditions of their development, on the one hand, and the doctrinal developments they underwent, on the other. We should bear in mind that we are not presenting these sources as they would be *per se*, but solely what they were *made to be*, through Islamic scholarship or contemporary social and human science.

The Quran and its Messenger

The word 'Quran' is the Anglicized form of the Arabic term *qur'an*, which refers to the notion of recitation. According to dogma the Quran is the form taken by the revelation that the Prophet received. Tradition reports that the first revelation occurred one day when Muhammad had gone to sleep after meditation exercises. The Angel Gabriel appeared to him, showed him a piece of brocade, and instructed him to recite. Muhammad answered: 'What must I recite? I have nothing to recite.' The first verses were then revealed to him:

> Recite in the name of your Lord Who created, created man from a clot of congealed blood. Recite: and your Lord is Most Generous, Who taught by the pen, taught man what he did not know.

The original matrix of the text was transmitted in fragments to the Prophet via Gabriel. A quotation from the Quran is therefore not attributed to Muhammad but to God. In its revealed form the Quranic text is composed of 114 *sura* predominantly organized in a decreasing order of length.

In the history of the Prophet there are two important milestones: the date of the Hegira, that is to say, of his emigration in 622 from Mecca to Medina; and that of his death in 632. Tradition has it that the Call, that is to say, the first revelation made to Muhammad, took place around 612. The Quran says that Muhammad lived among his fellow citizens for a lifetime, usually held to be a period of forty years, before beginning his preaching. This brings us, approximately, to the year 570. His father, 'Abd Allah, belonged to the clan of Hashim,[1] from the tribe of Quraysh.[2] He died before the birth of Muhammad, who was brought up by his grandfather, 'Abd al-Muttalib. His mother, Amina, died when he was only five or six years old and he was then entrusted to his uncle Abu Talib, the father of his cousin and future son-in-law, 'Ali. At the age of twenty-five he became the business associate of a rich widow, Khadija, whom he then married and with whom he had a daughter, Fatima. She would marry 'Ali and would give birth to the Prophet's only descendants, among whom were Hassan and Hussein, progenitor of the line of Shi'a imams.

It is recounted that Muhammad kept the revelation hidden from everyone except the original circle of converts:

Khadija, 'Ali, 'Uthman, and Abu Bakr. Historiography, whether Islamic or Orientalist, shows us that when it became public, Meccan preaching developed in parallel with resistance to the Prophet. Key episodes included the dispatch of the Prophet's Companions most under threat to Abyssinia; the conversion of 'Umar, Companion and close friend of the Prophet; the exclusion of the Hashim clan; the deaths of Abu Talib and Khadija; initial contacts with the people of Medina and the idea of emigration from Mecca; and the invitation issued by the people of Medina to the Prophet to come and arbitrate their disputes. In September 622 Muhammad left with his first Companions, the Emigrants (*muhajirun*), and settled in Medina.

During the ten years between the Hegira and his death, the Prophet reputedly transmitted twenty-four *sura*s in which his role as leader was affirmed. The verses of the Quran depict him as concerned to consolidate, organize, and defend the community of Muslims (*umma*). On his arrival in Medina, new problems emerged. These included the relations between the Emigrants and the Partisans of the Prophet (*ansar*) who subsequently rallied to his cause; the question of the economic subsistence of the Emigrants; the attitude to adopt towards the Jewish tribes of Medina; and the realization of an ideal of social justice. The framework of the society of Medina was profoundly affected, but without undergoing a complete upheaval. The text of the revelation became more adversarial towards the Jews on each occasion that Muhammad failed to obtain recognition from them as the continuator and the seal of the prophets. The year 624 seems to have been the year of the final break, when the decision was taken to turn when praying towards the Kaaba of Mecca – at the time a polytheist temple – instead of Jerusalem. This is generally considered a decisive moment in the foundation of Islam, henceforth instituted as an autonomous religion. The changes of 624 also opened the way for the inhabitants of Medina, anxious not to compromise the renown of their sanctuary, to join Muhammad's community.

According to later commentaries such as that of al-Tabari, the Quranic text, which is almost the sole contemporary source for the life of the Prophet, mentions a series of raids launched against the polytheists between 623 and 627. A victory was won at Badr in 624. This was a significant event: victory could be seen as proof of the support of God for Muslims while also demonstrating that the new community represented a threat for the inhabitants of Mecca. On the other hand, 625 saw a Muslim defeat at the hands of Meccan troops. The authority of the Prophet was paradoxically reinforced by this reverse, given that his opinion had not been followed in the choice of tactics. Victories and defeats were on each occasion accompanied by repressive measures towards Jewish tribes. During this period, Muhammad married several times, first to Aisha (daughter of Abu Bakr) and Hafsa (daughter of 'Umar), and thereafter to the repudiated wife of his adoptive son. This last marriage was authorized by a revelation which affirmed the absence of links of kinship with adopted children.[3] In 627 the Meccans underwent a defeat at the Battle of the Trench.

From this date onwards, historiography and translation show that the community was engaged in a process of expansion, with wider objectives. A revelation enjoins Muslims to make the pilgrimage to Mecca in 628. The Medinan caravan was intercepted, but a compromise was reached in the Convention of Udaybiyya. Muhammad abandoned the pilgrimage that year, but received a guarantee of safe passage for himself and the Muslims the following year. Several Meccans converted at that time, among them the two future leaders of Muslim conquest, Khalid ibn al-Walid and 'Umar ibn al-'As, who went secretly to Medina. In 629 the pilgrimage was well organized, and was a display of Muslim strength. The conversion of all the Arab tribes was envisaged. At the end of 629 the Udaybiyya Convention was dissolved and the Muslims embarked on the capture of Mecca. The Kaaba was made over to monotheist worship. Declarations of support – which did not necessarily correspond to conversions – multiplied, and numerous Arab tribes swore their allegiance (*bay'a*), among them the Christian tribes of northern Arabia and the Jewish and Christian tribes of Najran. They were permitted to freely exercise their religion in exchange for the payment of the tax (*jizya*) due from 'protected' people (*dhimmi*). Revelations multiplied against the impenitent polytheists.

The Tradition indicates that in 632 Muhammad directed his last pilgrimage, called that of the Farewell. He died on the thirteenth day of Rabi' al-awwal (the third month of the Islamic calendar) in the eleventh year of the Hegira, without a male heir. The rivalries between different factions were rekindled. The question of the Prophet's succession was raised, although no provisions had been made to formalize the succession. The theme of allegiance to the successor of the Prophet, the Commander of the Faithful (*amir al-mu'minin*), emerged. The term caliph, or deputy of the Prophet, appeared only under the Umayyads in the seventh century, and it would be retroactively applied by historians to those figures usually called the Rightly Guided Caliphs. The nature of the power that the sources reveal to us is religious only inasmuch as the community over which it is exercised has its origin in religion. The dogma seeks to be firm: authority has its source in God, who delegated it to his Prophet, and the caliph is only the successor. In practice, however, the power of the caliph seems to have been political and personal, delimited by the word of God, the example of the action of his Prophet, and also the consensual opinion of the Muslim elite. Although the legitimacy of the caliphs was religious in origin, their power was not religious. With the third caliph, 'Uthman, from 644 onwards, this power took on a monarchical form.

There are no sources on the life of the Prophet which date from his lifetime, with the exception of a collection of texts regrouped under the title of the Constitution of Medina, which sets out the relations between Emigrants, Helpers, and the Jews of Medina. The biography of Muhammad is, furthermore, the theme of two particular genres in Islamic literature, the tales of conquest and the deeds of the Prophet, in addition to the Prophetic traditions, which will be discussed in the following chapter. Another Islamic genre, that of the 'causes of revelation', is interested for its part in the circumstances that surrounded the Prophetic transmission of the word of God.

In 'Orientalist' literature one naturally finds numerous biographies which are broadly inspired by the narratives of the Prophet's deeds while criticizing their historical value.[4] Orientalist literature stands apart from its Islamic counterpart in the sense that it aims, at worst, to discredit the person of the Prophet and, at best, to interpret his preaching historically and sociologically, thus relativizing its metaphysical dimension.

The Quranic text: Mystical revelation or law?

Going beyond an initial acknowledgement which is as irritating for the believer as it is historically grounded, one should distinguish between preaching – that is to say, 'the intervention of a man who speaks, acts, is deeply conscious of the uncertainties in his milieu, announces upheavals, and gives them a meaning' – and Prophetic teaching – that is to say, a collection of 'moral, economic, and political laws, elaborated after the time of the Prophet and in function of the changes which he provoked, and which, retroactively, are attributed to the Prophet'.[5]

The question of the nature of the Quranic revelation is, even within the Muslim community, one where opinions contrast and diverge most sharply. For some commentators, the revealed text is mystical in character and cannot be read as prescribing rules of a juridical character.[6] For others, it is essentially the Law of God which ordains and forbids.[7] It is clear that the Prophet envisaged above all a religious reform and a moral revolution: 'His authority was not legal but for the believers, religious.'[8] If Muhammad was led to play a political role, that was the result of specific circumstances, and, in particular, the role that his settling in Medina led him to assume. 'One has to recognize that the sacred text is not *the* primary source for legislation and that this text has above all a liturgical function, which did not prevent it from being later invested with this legislative role.'[9]

The arrangement of the Quranic text, as established today, is highly heterogeneous. The organization is arbitrary, beyond the principal distinction between the Meccan and Medinan periods. A single *sura*, on grounds of affinity, can include revelations from different periods. The Quran includes 114 *sura*s of varying length (from 4 to 286 verses). It is, essentially, the size of the *sura*s that determines their order, from the longest to the shortest, with the exception of the inaugural *sura*, the Fatiha. The term used in Arabic to designate a verse (*aya*) means 'sign': the verse is a divine sign addressed to Muhammad, who never attributed to himself any miracle other than that of having passed on the revelation. The title of each *sura* presents the name, the number of verses in the *sura*, and the period (before or after the Hegira) of its revelation.

The *sura*s that seem to correspond to the initial period of Muhammad's preaching are short, composed of solemn oaths, with sonorous rhymes and exhortations to practise different forms of virtue. Their style recalls that of pagan soothsayers. Themes are juxtaposed: divine omnipotence, resurrection, the Last Judgement, the cataclysmic fate awaiting the damned, the Divine Creator whom humans must recognize and to whom they must turn in repentance, and the inimitable character of the Quran. These founding truths are part of Christian and Jewish traditions as well as that of the ascetics. In addition, there are multiple exhortations to monotheism. Revelation multiplies invective in proportion to the resistance it provokes. A period follows when new themes appear, such as the clemency of God and the break with polytheism. A number of homilies assume the form of a triptych, with a dogmatic affirmation, the story of the prophets, and a conclusion which is an encouragement to avoid the fate of the impious. The rejection of polytheism imposes itself as well as prophetic continuity, with

Muhammad sealing the cycle of the prophets. One can identify a third Meccan period with longer verses, a less hermetic style, and themes of divine charity and uniqueness, with their corollaries of divine omnipotence and human predestination, that are more emphasized. Contacts with Jews are attested by the allusion to alimentary prohibitions and the idea of monotheism fractured by human malice. There is a hardening of attitude towards paganism. The nocturnal journey of the Prophet to Jerusalem is mentioned.

The *sura*s of the Medinan period are undoubtedly marked by the role of adjudicator that Muhammad had been called upon to assume. In the name of God the Prophet gave out sentences, on the basis of the customary rules that prevailed in Arabia at the time. It is, however, here too a religious authority that he claimed. It is nevertheless problematic to affirm that the Quran sets out the stable framework and the precise workings of a state, whether ideal or actually existing in the world. At most only three or four revealed norms in the Quran can be said to have a political connotation. Thus the sole real power is that of God: 'All judgement belongs to Him' (Quran VI, 67). There are, however, holders of power who must be obeyed: 'O you who have faith! Obey God and obey the Messenger and those vested with authority among you' (Quran IV, 59). They must judge and command in all equity: 'Indeed God commands … when you judge between people, to judge with fairness' (Quran IV, 58), as well as to consult the

41

believers: 'So excuse them, and plead for forgiveness for them, and consult them in the affairs' (Quran III, 159). Generally, the Muslim community, 'the best nation [ever] brought forth for mankind' (Quran III, 110), must command the good and proscribe evil: 'There has to be a nation among you summoning to the good, bidding what is right, and forbidding what is wrong' (Quran III, 104). There is therefore a contradiction in affirming the inextricable confusion of politics and religion in Islam when one is faced with Quranic verses so few in number and general in character.

The revelations of the Meccan period mix different obligations concerning ritual, morality, and organization of the city. One can undoubtedly speak of the institution of norms, but not of a legal system. The emphasis is placed on behaviour, on the blameworthy character of certain forms of behaviour, and on the virtue of pardon. There is an injunction to judge with equity, to reject corruption, to avoid lying. Other elements include the need to establish written contracts, to call witnesses, to stand by one's commitments, to return goods held in deposit. In the same way, the Quranic prohibition of games of chance and usury constitutes a moral norm and not a rule, with its conditions of application and sanctions in case of its infringement. This is equally the case of questions relating to war, plunder, or family relations. In the cases of war and plunder, the emphasis is on the identification of those one should fight, the treatment of the vanquished, or the sharing out of their property between the

Muslim victors. Family relations are treated in general, but usually from the point of view of how to behave with parents, children, spouses, and slaves. It is only in a subsidiary fashion that the Quranic text stipulates some rules, notably with regard to inheritance. Some crimes are designated explicitly by the Quran, but sanctions are not organized systematically and often prove to be more moral than juridical. An element of doctrine affirms, moreover, that the application of Quranic punishments can only be envisaged in a morally ideal society, which is illusory in this world.

While the Quran does not map out the contours of a legal system, it has nevertheless been abundantly used as the principal source, or, more exactly, as the guarantee for doctrine of a juridical nature. This can be seen in the penal, procedural domains, as well as those of family, property, and legal obligations.[10] In the Quranic text one can find dispositions on the struggle against the infidels. Even the rules for the division of plunder are set out in a detailed manner. We have seen that in the field of politics dispositions are very general: obedience, consultation, arbitration. There are also rules that fix taxes and how these should be shared out. In criminal matters the principle of *lex talionis* is generalized, with its corollary of equivalence between the blameworthy act and its punishment. In parallel, the principle of the blood price, which authorizes financial compensation for physical damage inflicted and the abandonment of the punishment of *lex talionis*, is encouraged for homicide and physical violence. It is even made obligatory in case of violence inflicted in error. One can equally note the passage towards a system of individual responsibility. Certain interdictions make their appearance, whose sanctions are postponed to the next world (such as usury) or on the contrary stipulated in the Quran; the latter are called the *hudud*. They are: theft (*sariqa*) (mutilation); banditry (*hiraba*) (death, mutilation, or banishment); fornication (*zina*: includes adultery) (flogging); mendacious accusations of fornication (*qadhf*) (flogging); and alcohol consumption (*shurb*) (flogging).

Other Quranic dispositions establish rules of procedure such as the written recording of debts, the presence of four witnesses to prove accusations of fornication (a condition which is difficult to meet and which strengthens the argument that Quranic sanctions possess an ideal and unattainable character), and the recommendation that witness statements be used. With regard to the family the Quran is more detailed. It authorizes polygamy while limiting it to four wives. The waiting period[11] required of a woman between two marriages is reduced, and the gift made on the occasion of a marriage (*mahr*) is reserved for the wife and not for her family. Marriage based on the exchange of women between families is forbidden, while full adoption is proscribed and a form of guardianship is substituted. The practice of excluding women from inheritance is ended and repudiation is given a formal

44

framework. The power of life and death exercised by fathers over their daughters is abolished. Some further regulations concern property and, more precisely, contracts.

Compilation and transmission of the Quran

According to its text, the Quran is not only inspired by God, it reproduces literally the divine and eternal revelation, which is consigned to a tablet guarded in heaven by the angels. Muhammad is the instrument of a revelation transmitted literally to humans. The text of the Quran is thus, according to Sunni dogma, the Word of God, an attribute which is held to be coexistent with Him. It is uncreated, a miracle, an incomparable and inimitable work. It is nevertheless the case that Islamic dogma recognizes that the written and complete version of the Quran attained its definitive form not during the Prophet's lifetime but during the first fifty years of the Hegira. The revelations were memorized and recited, something perfectly normal at a time when a poetic and oral tradition was dominant. Undoubtedly fragments of the Quran were committed to writing, as an *aide-mémoire* in particular, but not in a complete and systematic fashion. What is more, the writing of Arabic was not totally formalized at the time, and divergent readings of the same text proved possible.

One can identify two series of important elements: those that concern the history of the written compilation of the Quran, and those relating to the organization of the text as it was codified at a particular moment. It is known in any case that at the time of the Prophet's death, the fear of a loss of the revelation led the first caliph, Abu Bakr, to commission a secretary to compile a written text based on private collections of verses of the Quran and consultation of the best 'bearers of the Quran'. Serious divergences at the time of the military campaigns underlined the need for an established text for the largest possible number. In 650 the third caliph, 'Uthman, had the text of Abu Bakr revised, corrected, and completed – but only taking account of the Meccan tradition, and with a result widely considered imperfect. Multiple versions followed, revising certain details of the text and improving various orthographical questions which enabled a more precise reading of the text. In any case, the establishment of the Quranic vulgate is an important issue, corresponding, at the end of the seventh century – that is to say, during the reign of the Umayyad caliph 'Abd al Malik (685–705) – to the first phase of institutionalization of Islam. This period also saw the building of the Dome of the Rock in Jerusalem; the minting of an original Islamic coinage, the representation of the caliph under an imperial form; and the development of the caliph as legislator. This process was not without difficulties, and the Shi'a denounced the manipulation of the Quran and contested the authority of the caliph to embody and make the Norm, authority which belonged in reality to the Shi'ite imam.[12]

Schools with different readings of the Quranic text emerged, but it acquired its definitive form from the end of the seventh century onwards. Today the text of the Quran is the same for all Muslims, even if the Shi'a affirm that the complete text will only be revealed at the end of time and the Kharijites[13] reject a particular *sura*, that of Joseph (Quran XII). In addition, the text is always vocalized, with the short vowels indicated, and so too the correct pronunciation and therefore the correct meaning, in order to avoid ambiguities. The text is divided into thirty equal sections, which enable it to be read over the course of a month. The establishment of a definitive form of the text signified the arbitrary conclusion of the debate on it and its variants. With the development of critical sciences, new readings emerged, which contested, among other things, the canonical vocalization, and therefore proposed new meanings for the revealed text.

One of the particular difficulties of the study of the Quran derives from the fact that, unlike biblical texts, it was constituted over too short a period to allow the text to settle into different literary strata. This renders it impossible to identify the different stages of the formation of the text.[14] Significant problems of chronology result, to which attention has long, although inconclusively, been drawn. Another difficulty associated with the analysis of the Quranic text is due to its status in orthodox dogma. A recited text of which knowledge by heart is presented, according to the Prophet himself, as an integral part of the 'real religion', the Quran is supposed to reproduce word for word a divine revelation which is eternal even in its formal aspects. The role of Muhammad is merely that of a docile instrument through whose agency the revelation was literally translated. Thus, for Ibn Khaldun (1332–82) the Quran is the 'Word of God revealed to his Prophet and transcribed on to the pages of the Book'.[15] In other words, the Quran was the Word of God, coexistent with Him, to which its miraculous literary form attested, according to a belief which doubtless developed around the second century of the Hegira. As it was a dogma, it was not surprising to see it contradicted by, among others, 'free spirits in Islam'.[16]

To the inimitability of the Quran was added its immutability. If the Quranic text amounted to the authentic and unaltered word of God, then it was placed beyond all possibility of interpretation. This question was the object of major debates such as that which opposed Mu'tazilites and Hanbalites in the ninth century. The former, known also as the People of Reason, held that the Quran was created, while for the second, the People of Transmission, it was the uncreated word of God. The Mu'tazilite tendency was defeated and the debate was closed. The hermeneutical project nevertheless developed in the twentieth century, due in part to the influence of critical scholarship among whose Muslim representatives one can mention Muhammad Arkoun, who judged it necessary to demystify the sacred text; Khalil Abdulkarim, who resituated the Quran in its historical context; Nasr Hamid Abu Zayd, who brought the Mu'tazilite theses up to date; and Abdolkarim Soroush, who suggested distinguishing revealed religion from its socio-historical interpretation.

Meaning and interpretation of the Quran

The Quranic text has been the object of an immense body of hermeneutic and exegetical work of criticism and interpretation. The established form of this work is *tafsir*, from the Arabic term for interpretation. More than mere commentary, *tafsir* relies on traditions, linguistics, and logic to help to clarify the meaning of the verses. Very many Muslim scholars have contributed to *tafsir*. Their work covers the complete Quranic text, and therefore includes the verses with a normative signification. To give an indication of the considerable margin of interpretation offered by the Quranic text, and the use that can be made of this margin, let us take these two verses of the *Sura* of the Women where it is said: 'Indeed God commands you to deliver the trusts to their [rightful] owners, and, when you judge between people, to judge with fairness' (verse 58) and 'O you who have faith! Obey God and obey the Messenger and those vested with authority among you' (59). Let us also consider three exegetes: Fakhr al-Din al-Razi, the epitome of classical Sunnism before the Mongol invasions (end of the twelfth century); Rashid Rida, the disciple of Muhammad 'Abduh, the leading light of Sunni reformism in the early twentieth century; and Sayyid Qutb, an important member of the Muslim Brotherhood and a founder of contemporary Islamism.

While Qutb makes the principle of equitable judgement a general principle or universal, imposed on all, and the basis of equality before God, Razi considered that only an imam can institute this justice and exert such authority, while Rida speaks of equitable judges, knowledgeable in rules inspired by God and capable of deducing them. It is interesting to note that, with regard to the sources of the Sharia, Razi establishes a fundamental distinction between what is regulated textually (Quran, Tradition, consensus), which has the value of an authoritative argument, and what is not (reasoning), which has only a derived value. Rida's only preoccupation is to insist on the equal value of consensus in the absence of a text. The most important question is determining the people whose consensus is sought and who hold authority. For Razi the People of Consensus are the *'ulama*, to the exclusion of all others. The holders of worldly authority are the amirs and sultans, when they act with justice and correctly, because in this case they obey God or – even better – the People of Consensus. Rida identifies the holders of authority with the leaders of the community and those who swear allegiance to a new ruler – in other words, the elite of the community. It is an example of the theory of representation according to which the consensus of these individuals is the consensus of the community, which makes it a duty to obey them. The reference to the Western model becomes explicit when Rida distinguishes the legislative, executive, and judicial functions.

Qutb is for his part a proponent of direct representation in the sense that obedience to the holders of authority is a mere logical consequence of obedience to God and his Messenger. To obey them is a derived and limited obligation, as each individual is ultimately the only guarantor of Law and Tradition. To sum up, whereas Razi invests the *'ulama* with the task of guidance and moral leadership of the community, Rida states that no one should be ignorant of the Law and that therefore the obligation is imposed on everyone. He sees in the monopolization of knowledge an incitement to elitism and popular ignorance, while considering that the function of transmitting knowledge must be reserved to a learned elite. Qutb, on the other hand, openly rejects the idea of any kind of learned elite, and speaks merely of an authority competent to 'pass legislation in an anticipatory way' with regard to certain behaviour which is potentially reprehensible. The revolutionary mysticism of Sayyid Qutb is symptomatic. It is an example of the politicization of Islam which propels religion into the domain of utopias.

Contemporary uses of the Quran

In the modern world the interpretation of the Quran has sometimes given rise to court cases, as in the famous Abu Zayd affair in Egypt. Abu Zayd taught at the Faculty of Arts at Cairo University. In 1992 he applied for promotion to the rank of professor. His application was refused on the grounds that he had attacked Islam and made declarations of doubtful orthodoxy. The affair developed further when a group of lawyers introduced a plea before the Court of First Instance requesting a court judgment to separate Abu Zayd from his wife, Ibtihal Yunis, also an Egyptian Muslim.[17] They claimed that Abu Zayd's publications 'contain elements of impiety which expel him from the Islamic faith … and lead him to be considered an apostate'. They asked that 'in the case of Abu Zayd the rules of apostasy be applied', which include 'separation of the spouses on the basis of a court decision'. In March 1995 the Appeal Court judged that it was 'the right of every Muslim' to 'combat evil where it occurs or promote the good where it has been neglected', and that it was legitimate to compel Abu Zayd and his wife to divorce on the grounds of his apostasy. While recognizing that Egyptian law does not authorize a court to judge the quality of a citizen's faith, the court affirmed that the situation is different when there is no doubt about a person's apostasy. With regard to this the Court made the Quran into the yardstick of the extent of impiety of Abu Zayd's work.

The Court declared: 'The author denies God the All-Highest his quality of Ruler as established by numerous verses … denies the existence of the throne and the angelic warriors of God, creatures attested by Quranic verses whose meaning is clear … considers that the verses of the Book of

God the All-Highest, if understood literally, form a mythical picture … he denies the existence of devils … denies genies the quality of truly existing creatures, attested in the Quran in verses whose meaning is clear … maintains that the Quranic verses do not constitute a reality nor a truth, but are rather an intellectual reflection of the prophetic period.' Thus, for the Court, Abu Zayd opposed the revealed Truth: 'The defendant, by what he has written, sets aside the words of the True God – may the All-Highest be blessed – by which He says in the Holy Quran, that He is the True God and that what He revealed is Truth, that He has not brought by His Hands or through His creatures what is vain, that the Messenger – may God bless him and give him peace! – does not talk in vain. The Book of God the All-Highest attests to these signs. The court relies neither on exegesis nor interpretation, to the extent that the Holy Quran constitutes the very model of a "text" requiring neither exegesis nor interpretation.'

The Abu Zayd affair shows that the interpretation of the Quran can be the subject of dispute, and thus become a matter of judicial and juridical importance. Between an attempt to renew Islamic hermeneutics and a purely literal reading, the interpretation of the sacred Text appears highly variable, fluctuating, depending on individual perspectives. The Quran, moreover, does not constitute a complete source of norms. At most, some judges can have recourse to it in order to confirm the validity of prevailing legal rules. These conflicts of interpretation of the Quran, seen as a source of legislation, contain a political dimension, given that the struggle to define authoritative interpretation is part of broader strategies of the exercise of or challenges to power. Referring to the Quran as the source of the Sharia moves from the circumscribed domain of the law to new territory, where more overtly political slogans are advanced, such as: 'The Quran is our constitution'. Such invocations of the Quran remain very vague in terms of substance, but are part of the tensions within Islamic societies and their reconfigurations in every sphere.

3

The Sources of the Divine Norm
Prophetic Tradition

The second of the sources for the knowledge of the Norm is the Sunna, the Tradition of the Prophet, which encapsulates the deeds, activities, and sayings of the Prophet and depicts the way of life of the Prophet, his Companions, and the first generation of Muslims. Although Tradition is undoubtedly ranked after the Quranic word in the hierarchy of these sources, it nevertheless constitutes, in practice, the principal source of norms which can acquire legal status. This prophetic Tradition has a complex history linking different threads of the Muslim community. One such thread is proximity to the Prophet, who instituted a system of authority within the community that he founded. A normative discourse was also established, whose themes derive from the Tradition while its effectiveness is based on an Islamizing of local rules: placing elements borrowed from societies subdued by the Arabo-Islamic conquests within a framework of Prophetic authenticity.

Establishing a community hierarchy and a corpus of norms

Unlike the Quranic text, which took on a definitive form at the end of the seventh century CE, the constitution of the Sunna was a lengthy process. The compilation of this major source only began around 720 under the Umayyad caliph 'Umar ibn 'Abd al-'Aziz (Omar II, d. 719) and culminated with Bukhari (810–70) and Muslim (821–75).

Two fundamental elements need to be taken into account in order to clearly grasp the dynamic of the elaboration of Tradition. The first relates to authority: the strength of a tradition concerning the deeds of the Prophet derives from the idea that an individual's authority is based on his proximity to the founder of the Community, Muhammad. The second concerns norms: the constitution of a corpus of norms for the Muslim community meant legitimizing the laws and customs of the various conquered territories by bringing them within the aura of exemplarity surrounding the founder.[1]

The question of the establishment of a new social hierarchy appears very early in Islamic history as recounted to us, and functions according to proximity to the Prophet. At the summit of this hierarchy are the first Companions of the Prophet, those who followed Muhammad from Mecca to Medina; these are the Emigrants (*muhajirun*). Thereafter come the supporters who rallied round the Prophet after his emigration (*ansar*). They were joined by those who subsequently gave their allegiance, most prominently the sedentary elites, notably those of Mecca, organized organically in tribes and lineages. The Muslim community grew in parallel with the Arabo-Islamic conquests. There was an aristocracy based on ethnic descent and rank, and a new class of indigenous clients who had converted to the Islamic faith of the Arab conquerors. In this vast movement which institutionalized Islam, genealogy took on a particular prominence. Whether a particular genealogy was true or invented, a claim of descent from a common ancestor is linked to the expansion of Islam. Such claims corresponded to a need for identity affirmation and demarcation as well as the legitimization of an authority that established norms.

The Tradition of the Prophet is in reality the principal source of rules and norms in an Islamic context. It fills out the relatively laconic character of the Quranic text and allows local practices and customs to be filtered through Islamic teaching, thus integrating the myriad contributions of local societies while avoiding centrifugal effects. It matters little that the Prophetic model of behaviour is the fruit of a later hagiographical construction. This is certainly the case, although it does not mean that a specific means of behaviour particularly associated with Muhammad did not develop across time. The exemplary status of the Prophet was the matrix for the elaboration of the Law, through the intermediary of the specialists, the *ulama*. Thus the time of the Prophet was no longer the distant period of origins, but a present-day foundational moment.'² The development of norms operated through a filtering of local elements, moving from the local to the universal, via the scholars and their knowledge of the deeds of the Prophet and the Arab environment of his preaching.

The science of hadith

The Sunna of the Prophet corresponds to the totality of the oral traditions (*hadith*) going back to eyewitness accounts of the life of the Prophet. The *hadith* is therefore a piece of information concerning his way of living, that of his Companions, and even of the first generations of Muslims. The tendency to give a particular weight to the period of the Prophet's preaching originated at Medina. The interest in *hadith* was not particularly limited to its regulatory capacity, at least in the beginning. It was more a question of shedding light on the circumstances of revelation and providing some keys for Quranic interpretation. It was towards the middle of the second century after the Hegira (*c.* 750) that Tradition study developed. For the Tradition scholars, it appeared that recourse to the Sunna of the Prophet could be an acceptable way to resolve a question not treated in the Quran. In the domain of normativity, the situation progressively polarized, between the supporters of the use of reason and the defenders of Tradition.

The general mechanism of *hadith* is that of the perpetuation of a memory through a chain of transmission leading to the witness of an event involving the Prophet, or which took place in his time. The *hadith* consists of two essential parts: the body of the text and the supporting chain of transmission. The body of the text consists of a short story recounting a deed or saying of Muhammad or one of his Companions. The 'support' is the means by which the *hadith* is identified, consisting of a chronological list of its transmitters. The principle is one of oral transmission attached to a direct eyewitness. The written version was a support, similar to a written reminder. With the passage of time the corpus of traditions assumed a considerable dimension. The tradition scholar Bukhari, in the ninth century, counted 7,200 authentic traditions.

The phenomenon of multiple traditions is explained empirically by a need to find 'Islamically correct' answers to new questions. Muhammad thus becomes the vehicle for legitimizing all kinds of solutions for problems that only emerged after his death. The causes of the inflation in the number of traditions are different, and are of at least three types. There were political issues arising from the struggle over the Umayyad caliphate in Damascus (661–750) which involved, on the one hand, the Hashimiyya, who considered that election and excellence could only proceed from belonging to the lineage of the Prophet, and, on the other, a certain number of non-Arab converts, whose objective was to put an end to the exploitation of populations ruled by the victorious Arabs. There are also dogmatic causes, associated with condemnation, attributed to the Prophet, of the opposing party in a controversy. Lastly, there are issues related to the emergence of Tradition as the first source of normativity, in opposition to local schools which favoured the use of reason. Jurisconsults invented numerous *hadith*s in order to support theses contrary to those defended by the Tradition specialists, who did not hesitate, for their part, to attribute to Muhammad statements that would confirm an opinion around which there was consensus. The result was an inflation in the number of *hadith*s, of which a high proportion were apocryphal, difficult to distinguish from the authentic *hadith*, and sometimes contradicted them. There were multiple reactions to this situation, ranging from a 'meta-hadith' affirming that everything circulating under the name of Muhammad could be attributed to him, to the circulation of counter-hadith intended to discredit *hadith* forgers. Those with a sense of irony viewed the multiplication of *hadith* with a considerable amount of scorn.

A method of internal criticism was developed by several *hadith* specialists; one can speak of a process of purification and selection. For a long time the only criterion for acceptance was conformity to generally accepted opinion. It turned out, however, that this was not sufficient to resolve the problem of contradictory traditions. Another risk was due to the way that traditions were associated with the names and authority of prominent personalities. It was thus necessary to question the genealogy of *hadith*, the chain of transmission establishing a connection with these personalities. The chain of transmission (*isnad*) was therefore the object of critical study. The solidity of transmission was a condition for the authenticity and validity of the content of the tradition. All the links in this chain had to be examined to see if the transmitters were morally irreproachable, unfailingly orthodox, and known for the quality of their memory. In addition, one had to examine the connection between the links in the chain (raising questions such as whether it is historically possible that a person could have received a particular tradition from the person preceding him in the chain), as well as the biographies of unknown transmitters. It was therefore possible to filter the corpus of Tradition by declaring numerous *hadith*s to be false or weak.

Several classifications were drawn up, according to the origin of the tradition, its renown, or the reliability of the chain of transmission. The first system of classification distinguished between the *hadith*s attributed to the Prophet as the interpreter of the divine will; those that recounted an action or declaration of the Prophet; those corresponding to the account of a Companion of the Prophet; and, finally, those attributed to the successors of the Companions. The second system is used in the Hanafi doctrinal school. It consists of accepting as *hadith* only traditions that were transmitted by several reliable chains in the same geographical area. The third system, the most widely used, organized *hadith*s according to their degree of acceptability.

First place goes to authentic *hadiths*, supported by an uninterrupted and unchallengeable chain of witnesses. Then there are 'good *hadiths*', with a trustworthy although not perfect chain of witnesses; and 'weak *hadiths*', with a weak chain of transmission. Some *hadith*s were considered forged, when the chain is very incomplete or when someone thought to be economical with the truth appears in the list of transmitters.

The establishment of this method of internal criticism did not resolve all the problems arising from the inflated number of *hadith*s, and, among other things, did not prevent competition between rival *hadith*s, some false and others true. Attempts were made to harmonize Tradition. The technique of abrogation (*naskh*) was of some help. This enabled a tradition dating from an earlier period in the Prophet's life to be abrogated by one from a more recent period. A coherent organization was therefore possible in terms of the content and context of the *hadith*. This compilation took place long afterwards, and was based on oral transmission, which inevitably raises difficulties of historical verification.

*Hadith*s were used primarily for religious purposes around the end of the first century after the Hegira (seventh century CE). It was only at the end of the third century after the Hegira (ninth century CE) that systematic collections and compilations appeared. Some collections classified traditions in terms of the reliability of the transmission chain: these are the *musnad*. Such a system enables the character and reliability of transmitters to be examined. Other collections include the whole range of subjects covered by tradition, for dogmatic, ritual, or normative purposes. In the context of their production, these collections aimed to demonstrate the capacity of Tradition to answer all questions addressed to jurisconsults. The *Sahih* of Bukhari and that of Muslim represent the perfection of *hadith* science.

The place of Tradition in doctrine and the science of its foundations

Tradition emerged as a result of the desire for a normative and uniform doctrine, marked by divine teaching and the figure of the Prophet. It was a reaction to the centrifugal forces resulting from the appropriation of political power by Muslims of Arab descent in the lands Islamized by conquest. Islamic expansion was accompanied by a need to regulate and systematize the rules governing lands and peoples under Islamic rule. Thus appeared the first groups of scholars or doctrinal schools at Kufa and Basra, and at Mecca and Medina. It is important to note that their legitimacy was dependent on proving a connection to a Companion of the Prophet: Ibn Masʿud for Kufa, Ibn ʿAbbas for Mecca, ʿUmar and ʿAbdullah ibn ʿUmar for Medina. ʿEach ancient school of law, having projected its doctrine back to its own eponym, a local Companion of the Prophet, claimed his authority as basis of its teaching.'[3]

Tradition scholars settled in most Islamic cities. They were vigorously opposed to any idea of reason and opinion in the definition of normative doctrine. For them normative doctrine had to be filtered through moral and religious principle, which they limited to Muhammad's actions and words. This way of proceeding had the force of authority: how could one contradict teaching going back to the Prophet himself? In practice, doctrinal schools assimilated Tradition and wrapped their ideas in its mantle. Under pressure from Tradition scholars there was some evolution of doctrine, but undoubtedly not to the extent to which the most zealous defenders of Sunna aspired. The main effect was to oblige a justification for doctrinal evolution to be found in conformity to canonical Tradition. This evolution was consecrated in the science of the foundations for knowledge of the Law (*'ilm usul al-fiqh*). This developed in the third century after the Hegira (see Chapter 4), following in the footsteps of Shafi'i. Only analogical reasoning was permitted, with Prophetic Tradition considered the supreme source.

Prophetic Sunna therefore becomes, if not the primary source, at least the quasi-principal source of normative doctrine, in both a restrictive and an extended sense. Restrictive, because only *hadith*s attributed to the Prophet were recognized, excluding those attributed to his Companions or *a fortiori* other individuals. This also gave doctrinal reasoning a retrospective direction, limited to a voluminous yet fixed corpus. It was 'extensive' in that it elevated Tradition to the position of principal corpus of doctrinal elaboration. With the help of the theory of abrogation, it was even possible to render impossible any contradiction between a Prophetic tradition and a verse of the Quran.

The Sunna as guarantee of authenticity and authority

The question of the uses of the Tradition goes well beyond its applications in jurisprudence or *fiqh*. Islamic normativity has been divided into Islamic law, on the one hand, and Islamic deontology, on the other. This accentuates the contemporary tendency to use Sunna in order to give foundation to, legitimize, or endorse a way of life, an ethical vision, a way of being and engagement in daily life. Tradition therefore becomes a basis for idealization of the past, and the life of the Prophet becomes a model for behaviour. The reference to Sunna and *hadith* became an authoritative argument. One can for example mention an Egyptian lawyer who stressed that the content of a rule is not as important as its register of expression. 'If you quote a *hadith* to someone he will say to you "May God bless him and give him peace!" showing that he knows that it is a word of the Prophet and that he has heard it a thousand times from the pulpit. If I convert humanly acceptable values into values which are culturally acceptable, I can guarantee that they will be better understood and applied, and also seen as constraining for people. If people feel that it is their law and their religion they will conform to it.'[4]

Tradition also offers a model of behaviour for those who seek their inspiration in Prophetic example. Every revivalist movement calls for the rediscovery of the Golden Age by the reproduction of practices current 'at the time'. The corpus of the Sunna is particularly suited to this exercise in all areas of life, whether personal or public: clothes, hygiene, sexuality, education, politeness, ritual, wisdom, psychology. It is an entire system of morality founded on right practice, a deontology based on an orthopraxis, itself based entirely on the imitation of pious ancestors, with the Prophet himself in prime position. An argument based on authority – 'There is no room for debate because that comes from the Messenger of God' – is thus supported by an argument based on imitation: 'It is correct because it is identical to what the Prophet used to do.' The believer who follows this approach does not have to understand the complexities of the Law or Divine Teaching: it is sufficient to adopt a procedure, a way of acting or being, which alone is sufficient to guarantee his integration into the world and his conformity to Islamic morality.

This re-enchantment of the world by a return to the Golden Age proceeds necessarily from an idealization in which critical methods play a small role, if any. Authority does not function hermeneutically, interpreting the corpus of Tradition from an evolutionary and dynamic perspective. On the contrary, it operates in a cumulative manner, with an aptitude for amassing knowledge that can statistically determine a stable world, down to the smallest detail. It therefore appears that, in the process of the invention of Tradition, the most important element is its idealization for normative purposes. All tradition is the product of a retrospective rewriting, aiming to establish a master document which is evidence of the truth of tradition, and from which all authority derives. In this way the authorized version of a way of acting, anchored in a foundational past, departs from history and is idealized, prescribing the norms for behaviour in a quotidian world which is decisively located in history and therefore contingent.

Contemporary legal uses of the Sunna

In addition to the Sunna constituted as a model of orthopraxis, one can note another usage which tends to give it a legal aspect. This evolution, at the level of the Sharia as a whole, will be the subject of another chapter. We shall evoke an Egyptian example which enables us to illustrate this tendency to make Tradition of the Prophet a juridical source.

In Egypt in July 1996 excision (female genital mutilation) was dealt with in a communiqué by the Ministry of Health which stipulated that 'the practice of the excision of girls, whether in hospitals or in public or private clinics, is forbidden, except in pathological cases authorized by the director of the department of gynaecology and obstetrics and on the decision of the doctor in charge'. In addition, 'the practice of this operation by non-medical personnel is a crime punished according to the laws and regulations'.[5] The communiqué was only the latest measure in a long history of unsuccessful campaigns against this practice. It nevertheless provoked a relatively animated debate in a society in which the practice is still widespread. In the same way as in the Abu Zayd affair, cited in the preceding chapter, and although the case was not brought against any particular person, a group of people introduced the case at the Cairo Administrative Court asking for the decision of the minister to be suspended and cancelled. Several arguments were invoked in order to support their case: the ministerial decision contravened the article of the 1971 Constitution which made the principles of Islamic Sharia the principal source of legislation; the agreement among jurisconsults on the legitimacy of excision as a Prophetic tradition – only discussing whether it was obligatory or recommended; the impossibility for the government to challenge a Quranic disposition or a recommended or obligatory rule in Islamic law. In its judgment of June 1997 the Administrative Court, having discussed excision in the light of Islamic law, and basing its judgment on a fatwa, ruled in favour of the plaintiffs.

The Ministry of Health appealed against this decision before the Administrative High Court, which gave its judgment in December 1997. The plaintiffs repeated their arguments. The Court's judgment was structured around several questions, including the extent of the power of the minister to ban customs justified by Sharia and Prophetic

Tradition, among other sources. The Administrative High Court observed the distinction made by the Constitutional Court between Sharia principles that are not subject to interpretation and those where reasoning can be applied. In the absence of any absolute rule, the Court says, in substance, that the legislator is authorized – and even required – to exercise his interpretative reason with respect to the time and place. With regard to excision, the question was the kind of rules that prescribed it. The Court underlined the absence of unanimity among jurisconsults and the weak character of the traditions invoked. It could not therefore be an absolute rule, and the intervention of a legislator was, from this point of view, perfectly legitimate. The Court added that the articles of the Penal Code of 1937 which specify that the dispositions of the Code do not affect laws based on the Sharia or which invoke it were not applicable to excision. This was not an obligation in Islamic law, whether absolute or relative. On the contrary, in virtue of the Islamic adage 'neither prejudice nor counter-prejudice', according to which a wrong cannot be righted by a greater wrong, the Court concluded by saying that excision is a practice proscribed by Sharia and positive law.

'Since it is medically established, in gynaecology and in obstetrics, that the reproductive organs of women are not, in the state in which God the All-Highest has created them, affected by illness, and is not a cause of illness or pain of any kind which could lead to a surgical intervention, it is therefore a highly sensitive matter to interfere with these natural organs. In the strict sense of a legal rule, excision does not constitute therapy for an illness, remedy for an affliction, relief for real suffering or the prevention of a future suffering, all things which would authorize surgical intervention. When this intervention does not meet an imperative health requirement or therapeutic need in the face of congenital affliction or pathological situation, it is considered illegal, when there is a lack of one of the conditions justifying the medical acts on which the right of the doctor or surgeon to treat the sick person is founded.'

One sees therefore how Tradition becomes involved in contemporary judicial debates. Its character, made up of contrasts, plurality, and occasional contradictions, makes it unable to impose itself in a univocal way. It has become the material source of contemporary law, but its composite nature makes it susceptible to uses of a moral, political, and even ideological kind. The case above is a good illustration of the role it has been made to play. As a source of exemplarity and identity, it has become a model of behaviour to believers. Tradition is above all a moral and normative ideal. All currents of thought which claim to reconnect with the era of the Prophet derive their inspiration from Tradition rather than from the Quran.

4

Access to Sharia

Consensus and Analogical Reasoning

The theory of the foundations of knowledge of the Law generally presents two sources which complement the Quran and Sunna. These sources are consensus (*ijma*ʿ) and analogy (*qiyas*). The status of these two subsidiary sources is very different from that of the Quran and Sunna. Alongside these two material sources, scholars recognized competent authority and a reasoning procedure. It is therefore unsurprising that they have provoked fierce debate. It is through these debates that doctrine was constituted into a remarkable corpus known as *fiqh*. The key elements of what one today calls Islamic law or Sharia are derived from *fiqh*. This developed in the effervescence of the urban centres of the nascent Islamic community, against a background of local custom, use of personal reasoning, tension with Prophetic Tradition, and the emergence of specialists called the *fuqaha*ʾ. Its principles are the basis of doctrinal consultation as well as legal judgments.

The development of doctrinal schools

Fairly early in the history of Islam, certain individuals, because of their ancestry and the authority derived from their personal rectitude, began to express their opinions about the rules to follow on the basis of local practice; progressively, this procedure was preceded by examination of the conformity of practice to Quranic rules. Analogy was the method followed, in a rudimentary fashion at first, with recourse to maxims.[1] Use was also made of local customs – at least in so far as they did not contradict the principles of the Quran and the incipient Sunna. It was in the principal cities of the Arab empire that these emblematic figures appeared, and were joined by disciples. Gradually they formed doctrinal schools. It is in reaction against this disparate collection of schools that Ibn al-Muqaffaʿ (724–56), the Persian author of the famous fables of *Kalila and Dimna*, put forward a compilation of rules presenting the advantages of homogeneity – the same rules for all – as well as a possibility of evolution – with the political authority having the power to amend them. He noted that 'there is no school which is not vain enough to believe in the superiority of its doctrine, disdaining all the others'. He added that 'the judge calls Tradition dispositions which are not part of it … basing himself on personal opinion, he is led, by attachment to his opinion, to give a point of view which is not shared by his co-religionists'. Finally he noted that in case of divergence 'it will be necessary to seek which of these groups is the most worthy of confidence and which interpretation is the closest to justice'.[2] Thus, in the middle of the eighth century one could observe numerous divergences, opposing doctrinal tendencies, and judges who called their personal opinions Sunna. It was necessary to seek solutions that gave priority to justice.

Progressively the specialists in legal doctrine grouped themselves in schools in Medina, Mecca, Kufa, Basra, or in Syria. They were distinguished above all by geographical and social factors as well as by a variety of customs and local habits. Iraq was the centre of the first efforts to systematize a properly Islamic normativity, which took Quranic rules into account while recognizing the authority of local practices and the importance of scholarly opinion, above all when it formed consensus. Practices were often validated by recourse to a doctrinal opinion attributed to a great figure of the past, himself connected to a Companion of the Prophet: Ibn Mas'ud in Kufa, Ibn 'Abbas in Mecca, 'Umar and his son 'Abdullah in Medina. This was the beginning of the process of projecting a living practice backwards into the Prophetic past.

Tradition science developed largely in opposition to the idea of local custom and individual reasoning. Tradition scholars argued that *hadith*s going back to the time of the Prophet should replace local custom. From a doctrinal point of view, this movement prevailed: it soon became no longer possible to oppose *hadith*s, only to perhaps interpret them or attach local custom to them. This did not, however, lead to the disappearance of the different schools, which, while recognizing the principles defended by the Tradition scholars, nevertheless continued to develop their doctrines. The recourse to reasoning continued, in the guise of an analogy with an institution or an existing decision, or that of an orientation towards a certain preferential conception of what is fitting for public interest. About halfway through the second century of the Hegira the 'literary period' of the schools began – that is to say, the writing down of their doctrinal elaborations, whose evolutions can, from that moment, be followed precisely. Doctrinal reflection tended to increasing elaboration, with recourse to Tradition and a mixture of logical, ethical, and religious dimensions. This process culminated with the jurisconsult Muhammad al-Shafi'i.

Consensus

As soon as doctrinal schools began to appear, reasoning and opinion became associated with the notion of consensus. Consensus among an influential group, tribe, or local community linked to the Arab rulers was often the basis for the creation of a custom. Consensus among scholars in the cities closely linked to developing Islam (in Arabia, in garrison towns, and certain regional centres) was particularly important. The people involved were men known especially for their piety and exemplary behaviour.

Their study of Islamic norms was sometimes linked to the practical exercise of the duties of a judge, but tended above all to be of a doctrinal character.

The principle of consensus emerged at a time when the choices of a group depended on family, clan, or tribal institutions which could be consulted for an opinion. As soon as the Muslim community went beyond the frontiers of Medina and the Arabian Peninsula, it became organizationally difficult to obtain the agreement of all Muslims. Two conceptions of consensus came into conflict: one was limited to scholars of a particular school or a locality, and the other required consensus among Muslims as a whole. In the second instance consensus concerned only questions of a generally uncontroversial nature such as belief in one God, the prophecy of Muhammad, or the performance of certain rituals. Doctrinal theories on the subject of consensus diverged, basically over the weight that should be given to scholarly opinion. While the practical result of the broadening of consensus to the wider Muslim community was to dilute consensus and render it ineffective, restricting it to scholars able to interpret texts gave consensus a real potential for innovation, but also rendered it vulnerable, for this very reason, to criticism by Tradition scholars for innovation (*bid'a*), which was seen as reprehensible. Shafi'i supported an extension of consensus, a view one can consider as negative in that it rejects local and limited consensus. The Maliki doctrinal school recognizes the authority of consensus among scholars at Medina, concerned essentially with customary practice among the early Muslim community. In general, the weight of consensus as a means of extracting doctrinal rules weakened as the authority of Tradition became pre-eminent and the creative capacity of local schools was curtailed.

Contrary to the Quran, which was revealed, and Tradition, which came from lived experience, consensus is a derived source based on the two first material sources, and on the isolated *hadith* in which the Prophet says that the community of Muslims cannot agree on an error. Consensus, so symbolic that it serves to define Sunni Islam (*ahl al-sunna wa'l-jama'a*, the People of Tradition and Consensus), had little impact on the development of Islamic doctrine, at least after the period of its formation in the large local centres.

Reasoning and analogy

Early periods of doctrinal development were marked by diversity for at least two reasons: the influence of local custom, and the use of personal reasoning. The latter sometimes took the form of preferential reasoning according to public interest (*istihsan*). There was no homogenizing central administration among the different doctrinal schools. The authority of rules deriving from personal opinion was consolidated as scholars from the same locality agreed on their content. This led to the compilation of dogmatic collections. It was precisely in reaction to this fragmentation that the Tradition movement developed, and finally imposed itself. As in every normative process, it was necessary to set out a framework, rules, and the margin of interpretation which was authorized. A mere Quranic reference could not suffice. 'The interpretation of the Quranic dispositions was largely a matter of personal discretion.'[3] This led to an increase in rather than a reduction of diversity. The preoccupation with homogeneity and coherence led to the substitution of analogical deduction for arbitrary personal reasoning. This was originally somewhat summary. For example, the amount fixed for a marriage dowry, considered as a compensation for the loss of virginity, was evaluated in comparison with the price fixed for the loss of other property of value.

Analogical reasoning (*qiyas*) is the fourth foundation of *fiqh*. Like consensus, it is a derived source. In theory it is only authorized where there is no consensus about a question, or if the question is completely new. Analogy is not a repertoire to which the jurisconsult can refer, but rather a method which enables rules to be deduced from other material sources. It is made up of four elements: the new case requiring a solution; the paradigm with a scriptural basis or consensus; the *ratio legis*, the common attribute connecting the new case to the paradigm; and finally, the rule proper to the paradigm which, because the new case is connected to it, can be transposed to the new case. 'The archetypal example of legal analogy is the case of wine. If the jurisconsult is faced with a case involving date-wine, requiring him to decide its status, he looks at the revealed texts only to find that grape-wine was explicitly prohibited by the Quran. The common denominator, the *ratio legis*, is the attribute of intoxication, in this case found in both drinks. The jurisconsult concludes that, like grape-wine, date-wine is prohibited due to its inebriating quality.'[4]

Reasoning occupies an essential place in the production of analogy. The common attribute between the new case and the paradigm is not always obvious. Adequacy and relevance can also come into play, supposing a complex process of reasoning independently of textual sources or consensus. For example, the jurisconsult can highlight that it is the harmful effect of hallucinogenic substances that makes the forbidding of narcotics relevant while there is no clear text on the subject – only a possible analogy with grape wine. However, reasoning cannot proceed in an arbitrary way; it is governed by the revealed basis of Islamic normativity and its objectives, namely to command what is right and forbid what is wrong.[5]

Other forms of reasoning besides analogy are permitted. This is true of the *a fortiori* argument which permits an explicit meaning to be derived from a disposition that denotes it. Even the argument based on preference can be accepted, as long as it can be attached to a consensus which, because it induces the certitude that the solution adopted is true, is equivalent to a sacred text. For example, in the case of ablutions carried out with ritually impure water, and following the logic of analogy, one ought to conclude that the prayer was invalid. The logic of the preference-based argument, based on necessity or emergency, among other things, enables the obstacle to be overcome, showing that the accomplishment of the prayer is more important than the inconvenience of the unclean water. Reasoning based on the general interest, as it underpins Islamic normativity in the areas of the protection of life, of the mind, of religion, private property, and progeny, was also considered a technique that could be a basis for a disposition to be declared adequate. These reasoning techniques are assimilated to analogy, although they do not in fact constitute analogy itself.[6]

Jurisconsults

Consensus and reasoning are secondary sources which enable the rules of the Sharia to be identified. This identification is carried out by individuals who initially appeared as specialists, progressively constituted schools, and contributed to the elaboration of doctrine. As previously mentioned, *fiqh* is not law in the modern sense of the term, but a doctrinal edifice produced by jurisconsults. At the base of this edifice is the idea that human understanding is necessary in order to mediate between the will of God and human reality, thanks to a capacity, the effort of interpretation (*ijtihad*) – that is to say, the process by which, in the face of an unprecedented situation, one can find a solution based on revealed textual sources or sources associated with the Prophet.

A jurisconsult able to give an opinion is therefore someone capable of producing the effort of interpretation, a *mujtahid*. Doctrine has formalized the required conditions for proficiency in *ijtihad*, but there is no authority exclusively competent to bestow this title. Anyone can, in practice, claim to be a *mujtahid*, and only the public reputation of the person will confirm it. The formal conditions are: knowledge of the normative verses of the Quran; critical knowledge of normative *hadith*s; knowledge of Arabic; knowledge of the theory of abrogation; mastery of the art of reasoning; knowledge of cases resolved by consensus (see Chapter 3). Once these conditions are fulfilled, the *mujtahid* has to exercise his faculties of interpretation in an autonomous manner, and thus not follow the opinion of another person, but only that which is founded on his own reasoning. In theory the *mujtahid* is taken as equivalent to the *mufti*, a person qualified to issue doctrinal advice. The latter does not take a decision, but provides advice on questions when applied to.

In doctrine, people who have not attained this rank are not allowed to give their personal opinions, and are bound to the opinions of a *mujtahid*. One refers to such a person as an emulator or adept (*muqallid*). There is a long list of intermediate categories between the adept and the master he follows. With time, many jurisconsults presented themselves as the emulators of a master or one of his first epigones, while in reality developing reasoning that went beyond the opinion of the *mujtahid* in question. This kind of adherence consists of affirming the authority of a solution, while giving it a more solid foundation. One can see therefore that it is in no sense blind imitation. It remains the case that in the immense majority of cases dealt with on a daily basis, it is the mere reiteration of the opinion of a *mujtahid* that prevails, in a routine and generally conservative manner.

The Sunni doctrinal schools

Islamic doctrine emerged from a movement of progressive elaboration beginning in the first third of the eighth century. We have seen how the first specialists appeared on the scene. They relied on local custom while seeking, with ever-greater insistence as time went by, to filter local custom through the Quran and Prophetic Tradition. These specialists created schools, in the sense that they represented the authority to whom the groups of jurisconsults referred. However, these groups often evoked the spirit of their pious ancestors rather than actually having recourse to their foundational work. The schools of Medina and Kufa were the most enduring of these early schools. On the basis of local customary norms and the prescriptions of the Quran and Tradition, and a review of local practice, a doctrinal corpus was constituted.

'It had originated in the personal reasoning or *ra'y* of individual scholars, but as time passed its authority was rested on firmer foundations. With the gradual growth of agreement between scholars of a particular locality, the doctrine was expressed as the consensus of opinion in the school.'[7] This tendency, in addition, had to appear as though it were not arbitrary but derived from a source contemporary with the Prophet, and, finally, from the Prophet himself. With the Tradition movement, the tendency accentuated.

Beyond doctrinal divergences, each of the two schools is characterized by a different mentality, which is due to the context in which they developed. While Medina was marked by a conservative attachment to Arab custom, the first scholars of Kufa in Iraq were distinguished by a type of progressive and speculative mentality linked to the formation of a new society which emerged from the Arab conquest outside the Arabian Peninsula. This is where Abu Hanifa (699–757), the eponymous founder of the Hanafi school, came from. His work is known for its qualities of reasoning and its logical coherence, but also for its disconnection from practice. It is difficult to claim that the Hanafi school is more liberal than others, but one can nevertheless state that its doctrine is concerned with individual freedoms – in the area of contracts, among others. It makes broad uses of subterfuges of reason. From Iraq, it spread to Syria, Central Asia, Afghanistan, and the Indian subcontinent. It became in a sense a 'state school' for the Seljuk and Ottoman Turks.

Malik ibn Anas (711–95) is the founder of the Maliki school. Born in Medina, he belonged to the Arab tradition which is at the heart of early Islam. He was known for his moral probity and his lack of self-interest. His teaching derives its legitimacy from 'Umar, the second Commander of the Faithful after the Prophet, and his son Nafi'. Attached to Prophetic Tradition, Malik showed himself critical towards *hadith*s coming from Iraq. The following quotation is attributed to him: 'In Iraq, you possess a *hadith* factory. They are composed at night and published in the morning.' A fundamental feature of the Maliki school is its attachment to Medinan custom – in so far as it represents the habitual practice of Muslims – to the general interest of the Muslim community, to argument based on preference, and its preoccupation with moral coherence. The Maliki school tended to move westwards, starting from its Medinan epicentre. It spread across North Africa, then in West Africa. It predominated in Andalusia.

Muhammad al-Shafi'i (767–820) is a central character in Islamic doctrine. Having passed through the principal centres of eighth-century Islam (Mecca, Medina, Kufa, Basra), he was initially a disciple of Malik ibn Anas. Heavily influenced by the theses of Tradition scholars, he was part of a context in which the process of the Islamization of normativity was completed. His essential contribution is methodological and epistemological: sources of doctrine, means of identifying norms, relations between the different

83

sources. His major work, *The Epistle*, can be considered as a source for the science of the foundations of doctrine (*'ilm usul al-fiqh*). Drafted during the last five years of his life, it seeks to achieve a synthesis of Tradition and reasoning. Shafi'i influenced the adoption of the Sunna as the corpus of traditions formally attached to the Prophet. Although second in relation to the Quran, the Sunna thus acquired a fundamental and autonomous status. The Quran must be read in the light of the Sunna, and not the contrary. In the same logic, if the Quran alone can abrogate the Quran (the Sunna can interpret the Quran, not contradict it), Sunna alone can abrogate the Sunna. The Quran cannot do it, as it must be read in the light of the Sunna. It is in the Sunna that one must seek a disposition to abrogate another disposition contradicting the Quran. With Shafi'i one observes an acceleration of the process of the formation of doctrinal schools. He was the founder of a school established on the principle of an exclusively personal master–disciple relationship. The school had a precise doctrine, reproduced, commented, and explained thereafter by his disciples. The Shafi'i school, starting from Cairo, spread to East Africa, and was also active in Arabia, Iraq, South-East Asia, and particularly Indonesia and Malaysia.

The Hanbali school began later. It emerged in reaction to the Mu'tazilite episode, which caused upheaval in the first half of the ninth century at the time of the Abbasid caliph al-Ma'mun. The Mu'tazilite doctrine maintained, among other theses often described as rationalist, that the Quran was created and not eternal. This provoked very strong reactions, both theological and political. Ahmad ibn Hanbal (780–855), who was above all a Tradition scholar, is one of the leading figures of the theological opposition to Mu'tazilism. Quietist from a political point of view, he considered Tradition to be the unique source of all doctrine. This led him to adopt a cautious position with regard to reasoning, and particularly preferential reasoning (*istihsan*). In his opinion even weak *hadith*s are preferable to analogy. This attachment to Tradition had a tendency to make Hanbalism the standard of conservatism and Sunni orthodoxy. The Hanbali school was not dominant in any particular territory. Its two main centres were Baghdad in Iraq and Damascus in Syria, under the inspiration of the reformer Ibn Taymiyya (1263–1328). It began a long decline, which was halted by Ibn 'Abd al-Wahhab in the second half of the seventeenth century, who revived it under the name of Wahhabism, based principally in Arabia.

Shi'ite doctrine

The origin of the principal schism within Islam is often attributed to the question of succession to the Prophet. On one hand there are the Shi'a, partisans of succession by blood and therefore through the line of 'Ali – cousin, first Companion, and son-in-law of Muhammad. On the other are the Sunnis, supporters of succession by co-optation within the tribe of the Prophet, the Quraysh. The historical reality is more complex. The succession to the Prophet was in fact controversial, above all with the coming of the third and fourth 'Rightly Guided Caliphs', 'Uthman (r. 644–56) and 'Ali (r. 656–61), who were both assassinated.[8] This led to the secession of the Kharijites, who rejected virtues attributed to birth rather than to ardour in fighting for Islam. Shi'ism did not explicitly constitute itself at this time, but later, in the second half of the Umayyad caliphate, as part of the Abbasid opposition, among other anti-Umayyad groups. Previously, nothing had distinguished dissident groups from one another apart from the political positions they adopted. It subsequently became necessary to consolidate the doctrinal bases of dissidence, which led to the affirmation of distinct identities.

Among the characteristics of Shi'ite doctrine is the principle of the sole legitimacy of the descendants of 'Ali through his marriage with Fatima, one of the daughters of the Prophet.[9] The result is a conception of Tradition restricted to *hadith*s connected to the Prophet through 'Ali and his descendants designated as imams. These are neither second-rank prophets nor representatives of the Messenger; they substituted themselves for the Prophet and assumed his tasks in his absence. Shi'ite imams are held to be infallible and free from sin. They are superior to all their contemporaries, and are the equals of Muhammad, but they have not been chosen to transmit the revelation. Around 874 the twelfth imam disappeared. He is believed to be hidden (in occultation) and no one can replace him. Knowledge of the plans of God is possible only through him. He will reappear at the end of time. In the meantime jurisconsults will exercise subordinate functions. Until the theory of government by jurisconsults (*wilaya al-faqih*) propounded by Khomeini, the spiritual guide of the 1979 Islamic revolution in Iran, there was no question of them exercising political sovereignty.

Another characteristic of Shi'ite doctrine concerns the use of reasoning. A famous controversy on this subject opposed two factions, the 'Usulists', who emerged victorious, and the 'Akhbarists'. The main issue was the use of interpretative capacity and reason. For the first group, interpretation was an indispensable method for the exercise of jurisprudential thought, while the second group rejected the use of any form of reason that could lead to a probability rather than a certitude. While the two tendencies agreed that analogy should be banned, Usulists recognized the fruits of reason as the fourth source of doctrine, after the Quran, the Sunna of the Prophet as filtered by the imams, and the consensus of jurisconsults, which included the opinion of an imam. For the Usulists the Muslim community was divided into two categories: those who could exercise their faculties of interpretation (*mujtahid*s), who alone were able to pronounce doctrinal opinion; and all the other members of the community, who could only follow the jurisconsults. For the Akhbarists only imams could be *mujtahid*s, while for the Usulists the obedience of ordinary believers to an active *mujtahid* was obligatory. This is the origin of the doctrine of the 'Referential Authority' on which the theory of *wilaya al-faqih* is based. According to this, the Referential Authority must exercise civil and religious authority, replacing the Hidden Imam across the whole spectrum of affairs.

The institution of the fatwa and doctrinal consultation

The impact of Islamic doctrine on the world and on society has been mediated through the institution of consultation (*shura*). It is through the person qualified to proceed with such consultations, the *mufti*, that doctrinal principles can provide norms for the ever-changing reality of the world. By definition, the *mufti* is a person capable of interpreting the sources of the divine Norm. It is not possible to know the Norm in its purity, and the jurisconsult can only communicate to interested people a qualified opinion on any given question.

The group of scholars authorized to give an opinion has become a class of professionals. Their action is essentially individual, and an opinion is not binding and is not accompanied by any coercion on the part of public authorities. Nevertheless, at a certain point the temporal authorities felt the need to promote certain well-known jurisconsults to the rank of official *mufti*s. In some places, there was one for each doctrinal school. In the Ottoman

Empire they acquired the title 'dean of Islam' (*shaykh al-islam*). The official status of these *mufti*s and their fatwas does not mean that they are superior to or exclusive of other opinions. At most they are sometimes considered, individually or collectively, as in the Moroccan Constitution of 2011, the sole interlocutors of state institutions and officials, or authorized to issue official fatwas.

Under various names, such as the People of Knowledge, advisers, and *mufti*s, the scholars of Islamic doctrine filled the role of experts in judicial institutions, with judges referring difficult cases to them. In general, judges seem to have respected the opinions of *mufti*s not because they were binding, but because they had the weight of authority. In Hanafi theory fatwas form the third level of Islamic doctrine. In reality they constituted the pre-eminent level, in all the schools.

Fatwas therefore occupy a dominant place in the development of Islamic doctrine. They were the subject of specific collections which regrouped all the opinions collected on questions of a new type – thus creating a precedent – and recognized as correct by the scholars of a particular doctrinal school. The doctrine of a school was elaborated by jurisconsults collating and organizing fatwas into compendiums. These tend to omit factual and personal details, sum up the questions and answers, and synthesize the doctrinal principles that emerge from it. These compendiums were engaged with their time, adding and removing cases according to their pertinence, in the opinion of the author, for the Muslim community.

The general principles deriving from these cases have filtered into manuals of the legal schools. The exhaustive collections have produced summaries to be memorized by students. A summary could therefore be authoritative for a school for some time, before another had to be drafted – which did not, however, make its predecessor obsolete. Doctrinal continuity was therefore assured.

The contemporary relevance of doctrinal reasoning

Islamic doctrine is characterized by its continuing relevance. In the twenty-first century there are institutions whose legal duty is to pronounce official fatwas, such as the 'Ulama Council in Morocco or the Consultation Office in Egypt. Religious authorities preside over these institutions, the Commander of the Faithful in the first and the Mufti of the Republic in the second. These institutions are often invited to give opinions on social or ethical questions, at the request of state authorities, tribunals, or individuals. One can observe in such a case how Islamic doctrinal reasoning proceeds in a contemporary context. By way of illustration, here are some extracts from an Egyptian debate.

The Mufti of the Republic, in October 1998, gave an opinion on rape and the rights of a woman who has been raped. His communiqué was followed by an interview stipulating the conditions that, from his point of view, legitimize the reconstruction of a woman's virginity. A few days later he gave an interview to a weekly newspaper in which he confirmed his positions. For the Mufti, a virgin who has been raped is automatically authorized to have an abortion before the fourth month of pregnancy. In addition, she has the right to ask a doctor to reconstruct her hymen. Finally, the Mufti recognizes that she also has the right to conceal from a future husband what has happened to her. The Mufti justified his position in the light of the fact that society does not sufficiently protect the security of women, and that one cannot therefore oblige the victim to assume a responsibility that would be hers only in ideal circumstances.

This example enables us to grasp how doctrinal reasoning engages with social reality. Virginity and the legitimacy of sexual relations are the basic components of the normality on which reasoning is based. With regard to sexuality this normality is founded on the relations established through marriage in an asymmetric relationship between men and women. Rape and adultery constitute an infraction to this normality. The reasoning of the Mufti functions in such a way as to 'normalize' the situation of a rape victim by authorizing an operation to preserve appearances and enable the woman to conform to the prevailing morality.

Beyond the Quran and the Sunna *fiqh* is the fruit of a complex elaboration developed by jurisconsults progressively grouped into schools. The image of a doctrinal construction that took on a fixed form in the Abbasid 'Golden Age' no longer stands up. Doctrine, on the contrary, has constantly evolved. At the same time, it has draped itself in the virtues of continuity, as it derived its legitimacy from its relationship to the time of Islamic origins. Sharia therefore was simultaneously profoundly conservative and capable of evolution, with the two characteristics conditioning one another. Evolution of the Sharia could not present itself as a break with the past, given that continuity with the past was part of its essence. Conservatism could not restrict itself to immobility, unless it resigned itself to drifting away from society.

5

A Survey of Doctrine

Having raised a number of questions about the sources of *fiqh* and followed the history of how it was constructed and the concomitant debates, we should now examine its content. In the light of previous chapters, it will easily be understood that the substantial rules of Islamic doctrine do not constitute a monolithic collection. From Shi'ism to Sunnism, from one school to another, depending on scholars, doctrinal elaboration offers important nuances, even basic differences. Across time it is modified, but it is a dynamic of evolution rather than rupture.

Classically, Islamic doctrine distinguishes acts of devotion, which organize the relations between individual people and God, and transactions, which govern the relations between people in a horizontal way. In this latter register, one distinguishes between the rules that cover family relations, property, contractual questions, and criminal matters. Political issues are often dealt with separately, in the same way as those relating to tax or the conduct of jihad. Within these broad subdivisions there are many variations, which are a function of the schools and their historical and geographical evolutions.

The classification of acts, hierarchy of sources, and capacity

A treatise on the foundations of doctrine is organized essentially around three questions: the nature of the divine Norm and the status of human acts; the ways in which the Norm can be known; and the relation between the believer and the Norm. Authors' ways of dealing with these questions vary, but the contemporary tendency is to follow the structure of the works of the great masters such as al-Ghazali (1058–1111).[1]

The divine Norm is presented as being the totality of the commandments to which people are subject, at every time and in every place. Denying this Norm is an irreligious act, or one of apostasy (*ridda*), something far worse than not being a practising believer. The constraints arising from necessity justify non-fulfilment of a prescription. The acts assigned to humans are classed in accordance with those to whom rights are attributed. On the one hand, there are the rights of God, which concern worship and a whole series of prohibited acts – including fornication and the consumption of alcohol, for example – and, on the other, transactional rights that concern family relations: property or inheritance, for example. Finally, there are rights applying to both God and humankind: Quranic sanctions or the blood-price, for example. Human acts are also classed in five categories, according to their intrinsic quality, independently of circumstance. First are obligatory acts which are themselves divided into obligations imposed on all people, such as prayer, and those on the community and whose accomplishment by one person is valid for everyone, as in the case of jihad. Second, recommended acts, such as feeding a poor person. Third, authorized but neutral acts, such as sleeping. Fourth, at the other end of the spectrum, one finds acts that are reprehensible but not forbidden, such as repudiation. Fifth, forbidden acts, such as theft, fornication, or banditry. Finally, human acts are also classed according to their relation to other acts. In this way distinctions are made between apparent and real causes, reasons and motives, obstacles and conditions of validity, nullity, or dispensation.

The science of the foundations of doctrine (*'ilm usul al-fiqh*) has put together a sophisticated methodology which enables rules derived from the sources of doctrine – both substantial (Quran and Tradition) and secondary (consensus and analogy) – to be identified and defined according to their degree of clarity, their value as proof, any secondary applications that can be made of them, and the order in which they are abrogated, in cases of contradiction.

A third question which is often examined in treatises on the foundations of doctrine is that of the relation of the believer to the divine Norm. The question of capacity is dealt with here, as well as that of the conditions required to exercise the ability to interpret in doctrinal questions. The central notion with regard to capacity is that of the person for whom the Norm is intended, the person whose task it is to realize it. The faculty of discernment is the first condition of capacity, on the basis of which a typology of limitations is elaborated; a child at the time of conception possesses rights but not duties, a young child has the capacity to enjoy rights under the guidance of his tutor, the infant endowed with reason possesses part of the capacity of exercise, and the pubescent child has more or less complete capacity. A typology of obstacles to capacity is also suggested, by which the status of the mentally disturbed, the retarded, the spendthrift, or the senile is fixed. Obstacles of human origin are also distinguished, depending on whether they are the result of licit circumstances, ignorance, error, or constraint. Some capacities are reduced, such as those of women, slaves, or non-Muslims. Finally, in this section, the qualities necessary for the exercise of interpretation are defined.

Pillars of the faith and acts of ritual devotion

Treatises on doctrine always discuss in the first instance the five pillars of the faith: the profession of faith (*shahada*); prayer (*salat*); charity (*zakat*); fasting (*sawm*); and pilgrimage (*hajj*) – to which a certain number of other acts of ritual devotion can be added. The double profession of faith, through which the believer attests that 'there is no God but God and Muhammad is His messenger', is not dealt with separately. Prayer, on the other hand, which constitutes the second pillar but the first of the acts of devotion, constitutes a section that is always extremely detailed. It must be distinguished from personal oration. The number of daily prayers was only gradually set at five: midday, afternoon, sunset, night, and dawn. This obligation concerns every adult Muslim of sound mind, but some circumstances, such as travel, can constitute a dispensation. Prayer must be accomplished in a state of ritual purity, is accompanied by a codified number of prostrations, and is oriented towards Mecca. Prayer can be undertaken anywhere, and may be carried out individually, but there is a preference for collective performance of prayer in a prayer room. On Friday the midday prayer is replaced by congregational prayer in a mosque, preceded by a liturgy consisting of prayers of praise, recitations, and a sermon. Certain particular moments, such as the end of the month of fasting, eclipses, or periods of drought are associated with specific prayers.

The third pillar of faith and second act of ritual devotion, almsgiving, evoked the notion of the gift of the superfluous. Doctrine formalized its rules, and, because of the difficulties of collection, it became a complementary tax. It is intended for eight categories of people: the poor and needy, agents who have the responsibility to collect the tax, converts to Islam, slaves, debtors, those who fight in God's name, and travellers prevented from reaching their destination. A special gift of alms is foreseen at the end of the fast, for the benefit of the needy. Today this act constitutes a voluntary obligation which is left essentially to the judgement of individual believers.

Fasting constitutes the fourth pillar of the faith and the third of the acts of devotion. It was in 624 CE that the Prophet instituted the month of fasting, which corresponds to the month of Ramadan of the Islamic calendar. Other periods of fasting are recommended but not obligatory. As the Hegira calendar is lunar, the period of fasting advances by about twelve days for each year of the solar calendar. It takes place between two new moons, from the appearance of the first crescent moon to that of the next. These points in time have to be established by direct observation. Fasting consists of complete abstinence from food, drink, and sexual relations from dawn until sunrise. This is an obligation for every healthy adult Muslim. Ritually impure women are barred from fasting, and have to recover missed fasting days later on. The elderly are also excluded, as are those engaged in heavy labour, pregnant or breast-feeding women, also with the duty to catch up the days during which they were obliged to give up the fast. During the month of Ramadan, supplementary prayers are encouraged, as well as a complete reading of the Quran. The end of Ramadan is marked by collective prayer at dawn on the first day of the following month, and by the feast of the breaking of the fast. The practice of the Ramadan fast is one of the most widely observed devotional acts, because of its collective and social dimension.

The pilgrimage to Mecca constitutes a particularly intense moment of Islamic ritual practice. The fifth pillar of the faith, and fourth devotional act, the pilgrimage, consists of visits to different holy places, including the Kaaba, a cube of masonry whose construction is attributed to Abraham. The Kaaba is covered in black material which is renewed each year, has a black stone mounted in its corner, and is flanked by the spring of Zamzam and the tomb of Abraham. Today the Kaaba is linked by covered galleries to the two mounds of Marwa and Safa. As a sanctuary consecrated to the one God, it is the site of circumambulation by pilgrims. According to Islamic doctrine the accomplishment of the pilgrimage is an obligation for adult Muslims of sound mind at least once during their lives, if their material circumstances permit it. Accomplishing the pilgrimage is an act governed by precise regulations, entailing conditions of purity and sacralization in terms of ritual and dress. There are two distinct pilgrimages, which can be accomplished separately or in combination. The *'umra* can take place at any time during the year, and consists of circumambulation around the Kaaba and the race to the mounts of Safa and Marwa. The *hajj* proper, which takes place each year between the eighth and thirteenth days of the month of Dhu al-Hijja, consists principally of a visit to the plain of Mina, another to the plain of 'Arafa, a halt on the mountain of the same name, a visit to the plain of Muzdalifa, the stoning of pagan idols, and an animal sacrifice. This takes place on the day of the Feast of the Sacrifice, in communion with the broader Muslim community. The pilgrimage ends with rites of return to normal life and three days of personal sanctification during which the only obligation is to stone three pagan steles. Visits to the tomb of the Prophet in Medina are not part of the *hajj*, but constitute an important moment for the majority of pilgrims.

One can also mention among the acts of devotion the rules of ritual purity. Quranic prescriptions on this subject are relatively few, undoubtedly because Islam did not depart in any particular way from the taboos that already existed in Arabia. Islamic doctrine developed a very precise casuistic reasoning on the subject, distinguishing, among other things, incidents of minor and major impurity, their sanctioning and reparation through ablutions. Dietary prohibitions have their origin in this same notion of purity. In theory everything considered as comestible is authorized. Prohibitions are relatively simple and not numerous in Sunni doctrine. They principally concern meat: pork, blood, and scavengers. Ritual slaughter renders licit (*halal*) the consumption of meat that is religiously authorized. Ritual slaughter can be performed by every adult Muslim of sound mind, cutting the animal's throat and invoking the divine name.

Other doctrinal prohibitions are more concerned with the Muslim's relation to God than with transactions between people. These concern the wearing of rich clothes and the use of gold and silver. They also forbid the representation of living beings, on the grounds that God alone has the power to create beings endowed with life. The prohibition of games of chance is part of the same category. In the Quranic text it concerned only a specific game, but it was subsequently extended to all forms of betting, including betting on races and armed combat. In the same spirit, doctrine forbids contracts whose object is not clearly specified.

Certain practices linked to dress have received doctrinal status. Among them is the wearing of the veil by women. Two Quranic verses concern female dress: 'O Prophet, say to thy wives and daughters and the believing women, that they draw their veils close to them'[2] and 'And say to the believing women, that they cast down their eyes and guard their private parts, and reveal not their adornment save such as is outward; and let them cast their veils over their bosoms.'[3] The meaning of these terms is relatively uncertain and therefore offers a broad space for interpretation. The concern is one of 'protecting that which is part of women's personality, avoiding only provocative exhibition … far from the broad interpretations of custom'.[4]

Other ritual practices, such as circumcision, have also acquired doctrinal status. The Quran says nothing specific about it, doubtless because it was a widespread custom in Arabia. It is nevertheless one of the most generally followed practices in an Islamic context. On the other hand, female excision is controversial, and its practice is restricted to some geographical zones. Death is also the subject of doctrinal rules. Islamic practices are rather simple: washing the body, funeral prayers, and rapid burial.

Family relations

A work of doctrine necessarily deals, in addition to devotional practices, with transactional acts (*mu'amalat*) – first of all, dispositions relating to the family. One finds rules relating to marriage, divorce, descent, and succession. This field shows *fiqh* in its broad and complex subtlety. It is not possible to describe it fully, and one can at most sketch out the broad categories developed by jurisconsults, which structure what contemporary legal language calls 'personal status'.

Although seen as the cornerstone of society, marriage, technically speaking, is only a contract in the strict sense of the term, governing the aspects relating to the provision of services. Marriage is also recommended for all those of an age to experience sexual desire. In Sunni doctrine it is seen as a contract intended to be permanent. On the other hand, Shi'ite doctrine accepts the principle of marriage for a limited period. The minimal conditions for marriage are the existence of two contracting parties, an offer and its acceptance, two witnesses who attest to the validity of the act, and the guardian of the female partner – namely her father, or, in his absence and by order of precedence, a male parent among his ascendants or descendants.[5] The consent of the female partner is required, except for the Hanbali, who authorize the father–guardian to act alone. In any case, the interests of the female partner should be protected in terms of compatibility of status (the socio-economic condition of her spouse), personal compatibility (her spouse's age and health), and material compatibility (her spouse's ability to pay the immediate and deferred marriage gift).[6]

Two male witnesses or a male witness and two female witnesses are required. They must be free, Muslim, adult, and of sound mind, and must ensure the public character of the marriage.[7] Concern with the public character of marriage explains why a marriage ceremony at a mosque, although not a requirement, is preferred by the Maliki. The marriage gift (*mahr*) constitutes an important element of the marriage. It is generally composed of two parts. One must be paid immediately by the male partner to the female, and the other is deferred, often until a divorce occurs. The gift, once paid, is the exclusive property of the wife, and cannot be symbolic. If the gift is not stipulated in the contract or is undervalued, the wife can ask the judge to decide on an appropriate amount for people of her rank. Polygamy is permitted: a man may have up to four wives, although the jurisconsults consider monogamy as preferable. Different impediments to marriage exist, such as consanguinity or kinship through marriage, excessive socio-economic disparity, difference of religion (a Muslim woman cannot marry a non-Muslim man, a Muslim man cannot marry a pagan woman), and the waiting period during which a widow or divorced woman cannot remarry.

Marriage entails the cohabitation of spouses, sexual relations, and the right of the female partner to be maintained in terms of lodging, clothing, and food commensurate with her socio-economic status. The contract can stipulate particular conditions such as an increase in the marriage gift, a specific choice of residence for the married couple, and the dissolution of the marriage if the husband contracts a polygamous marriage. Some contractual stipulations are invalid (for example, establishing that no marriage gift will be paid), but they do not affect the contract as a whole. A husband has the right to sexual relations with his wife, and to her obedience – on condition, however, that he fulfils his obligations. Each spouse has a right to inherit from the other, according to specific rules, but their respective belongings remain their individual and exclusive property. Failure to respect these rights and obligations opens up the possibility of recourse to a judge.

The dissolution of marriage is a no less important chapter of every treatise on the subject. Marriage ends automatically with the death or apostasy of one of the spouses. There are also different ways of breaking a marriage, the best known undoubtedly being the repudiation of a wife by her husband, a unilateral right reserved to men. To be effective, a statement of repudiation (*talaq*) must be pronounced three times, in unequivocal terms, either all at once or spread over three months, during the wife's period of menstrual purity.[8] Until the third declaration the repudiation is temporary, and the husband can give up. When three declarations have been made the repudiation is definitive, and the resumption of married life is impossible even if the repudiated wife has not remarried in the meantime. Once definitive, repudiation entails the obligation to pay the deferred nuptial gift. The first declaration of repudiation opens a waiting period of three menstrual periods during which the wife cannot remarry. This period is prolonged until childbirth in the case of pregnant women. Husbands are required to pay a maintenance allowance to their wives during the waiting period.

There are other ways to end a marriage, such as repudiation at the request of the wife and judicial repudiation. The first is an offer made by a wife to her husband to repudiate her in return for her renunciation of all the material benefits she obtained from her marriage (marriage gift and maintenance allowance). If the husband accepts this offer he must pronounce the formula of repudiation once. As for judicial repudiation, it can occur at the request of a wife in cases of serious ill-treatment, desertion by her husband, prolonged absence, lack of provision for her maintenance, or violation of the additional stipulations of the contract. Let us note, finally, that the marriage can be annulled by a judge if one of its substantial conditions has not been respected. There can also be an annulment if an error comes to light about the qualities of the husband, if constraint has been used, or if a grave incapacity (such as the impotence of the male partner) manifests itself. The marriage gift must be paid in full if the union has been consummated.

The legal status, care, and maintenance of children also occupy a central place. Children born to a married woman are considered children of that marriage. A child whose conception becomes apparent during the waiting period after the death of a husband or the repudiation of a wife is presumed to be the legitimate child of that man. Children born outside marriage are considered illegitimate. Therefore there is no recognized link between these children and their natural fathers. On the other hand, the birth of a child creates a legal relationship between child and mother. The birth of a legitimate child creates a duty of maintenance for the father. In addition, the mother has an absolute right to custody of young children – the age limit varies from one school to another. If a mother is unable to care for children, the duty can devolve to women in her extended family, according to an established order. Supervision of children's property until they come of age is the responsibility of the father.[9]

Inheritance constitutes one of the most detailed and complex chapters of every doctrinal work. The fundamental principle in this area is the distinction between agnatic heirs – in the male line – and heirs identified by the Quran. Each Quranic heir receives a share (half, quarter, eighth, third, two-thirds, sixth) of the inheritance, which varies depending on the existence or otherwise of other Quranic heirs. Inheritance applies after death or apostasy. The calculation is thus made that, if a son exists, he will receive the principal part of the inheritance, and if he has a sister, he will always receive the double her share. Without going into the details, let us note that technical solutions are provided by doctrine to situations that would be mathematically impossible or gravely damaging to one or other of the heirs.

Property and contractual relations

The notion of a contract does not constitute a specific section of the treatises of doctrine, but is present in all the dispositions relating to transactions, including those of a financial and commercial type. In general, a contract assumes that there are contracting parties who have attained their majority – minors and those disqualified for various reasons must be represented – offer and acceptance, and an object of the contract. The offer can be withdrawn before its acceptance. It is also possible to stipulate a right to terminate the contract. The contract requires the mutual satisfaction of both parties and the absence of fraud and unjustified enrichment. The object of the contract cannot be fundamentally uncertain, because that would mean it being explicitly forbidden by the Quran.

A specific series of contracts is recognized by doctrine. The most well known is, naturally, a contract of sale, in which a thing is exchanged through compensation of an equivalent value. Another form of contract concerns the sale of an object which will be delivered at a future date. The terms of partnership cover co-ownership and contractual association. A particular form of partnership, sponsorship, corresponds to certain aspects of what is commonly termed 'Islamic finance'. It consists of a partnership on the profits generated by a given property. Doctrine also regulates many other forms of contract: rent, loan, gift, guarantee, and procuration.

With regard to property, Islamic doctrine has established a complete typology distinguishing property of value from that without value, fungible and non-fungible property, productive and non-productive property, movable and immovable property. In terms of ownership, the rights of use and disposal are also distinguished. Ownership is distinct from possession. In instances of co-ownership each of the parties has a right of pre-emption on the share of his co-owners which is put up for sale.

Particular mention must be made of an act through which property is withdrawn by its owner from free circulation. By this act of immobilization or mortmain (*waqf*, *habus*) the owner can render a person (family or private *waqf*) or a religious or humanitarian institution (public *waqf*) the beneficiary of the usufruct of a property.

The *waqf* is maintained by a remunerated administrator and established in perpetuity, but is subject to conditional suspension or dissolution. The *waqf* passes out of the ownership of its initial owner and benefits its recipients for the duration of their existence. The *waqf* can in theory be eternal if the line of its beneficiaries is conceived in such a fashion that it will have no end. *Waqf* has been used to avoid the break-up of land holdings, disinherit certain categories of heirs, or avoid tax and expropriation. Private *waqf* has undergone a phenomenal expansion. This expansion removed from economic circulation a considerable proportion of immovable property, as much as half the arable land in nineteenth-century Algeria. Expansion led to a thorough and systematic reform of the regime, taking in general the form of restrictions on family *waqf* and incorporation of public *waqf* into the property holdings of the state.

Offences against life, the body, and property

Islamic normativity is outside the concept of law as it is usually understood at the present time. This is particularly true of the notion of criminal law, which is the focus of imaginings on the Sharia. Islamic doctrine is underpinned by the idea of compensation for offences against life, the body, and property, understood as a settling of accounts between the offender and the person who has been offended.[10] This is true of vengeance as well as financial indemnity whose object is not so much punishment as the reparation of a loss. Some of these offences are described and framed by the Quranic text: these are the 'limits' (*hudud*) prescribed and sanctioned in a fixed manner by God. All other offences, for their part, belong to the category of offences liable to discretionary punishment.

Under the appellation of *hudud* one can find fornication, defamatory accusations of fornication, consumption of alcohol, theft, and banditry. For the Shafi'i, retaliation for homicide or injury is added, and for the Maliki, insurrection and apostasy. Contrary to received opinion, the application of *hudud* is, from a doctrinal viewpoint, extremely restricted in nature. A Prophetic *hadith* specifies that the least doubt must exclude the application of *hudud*. It is not an exaggeration to say that *hudud* relating to fornication and theft are subject to conditions of proof such that, in the absence of a confession, it should not be possible in theory to apply this kind of punishment.

Fornication is defined as a sexual act involving penetration between completely capable persons, outside marriage and to the exclusion of any doubt. Doctrine distinguishes two forms of fornication: the first is committed by married adults outside their respective consummated marriages. A punishment of death by stoning is applied. A second is that committed by persons who are not engaged in such marriages, and in this case the punishment is one hundred lashes. To determine that fornication occurred, the evidence of four adult males must be given during a single hearing, stating in an extremely detailed and unambiguous way that they saw the couple engage in a sexual act during which the man penetrated the woman. To be admissible, a confession must be repeated four times and must be freely made. Homosexual fornication is dealt with in the same way as heterosexual fornication except in Hanafi doctrine. The pregnancy of an unmarried woman is equivalent to proof of fornication, although for most schools the accusation is set aside if rape is invoked. A defamatory accusation of fornication constitutes a second offence of the same type, and can be prosecuted independently of any legal action undertaken by the victim. It is sanctioned with eighty strokes of the whip unless the person responsible for the defamation produces four male witnesses who attest to the truthfulness of his accusation. Only a woman's husband can accuse her of adultery with impunity, although this accusation does not lead automatically to the application of the punishment for fornication, but only to the dissolution of the marriage.

Theft, to be considered one of the *hudud*, has to meet several conditions. It must involve the surreptitious appropriation of the property of others; the stolen property must be of a licit nature and unperishable, with a certain value; the stolen property must have been placed in a safe, protected place; the thief must have attained his majority and be aware of the precepts of Islam; there must be no doubt that the stolen property does not belong to the thief and that the thief is not a poor person stealing food. If not all these conditions are met, the theft belongs to the category of offences left to the discretionary appreciation of the judge. The penalty consists of the amputation of the right hand. A repeat offence is sanctioned by the amputation, successively, of the left foot, the left hand, and the right foot. Two witnesses must attest to the offence. A false accusation is condemned and is liable, in the case of malicious intent, to the punishment that is prescribed for thieves. Banditry also belongs to the category of *hudud*. It covers armed robbery, and the sanction is a reinforced version of that which applies to theft.

The consumption of alcohol is considered to belong to the *hudud* by most doctrinal sources despite the fact that it is not stipulated in the Quranic text. The accusation must be supported by two male witnesses or the confession of the person committing the offence. The punishment varies from forty to eighty lashes, according to the doctrinal school. The Malikis also class apostasy (*ridda*) among the *hudud*. It consists of denying the truth of the Quran, declaring the Prophet to be a liar, cursing God, Muhammad, or one of the recognized prophets, abandoning the principle of prayer, rejecting of a question established by consensus, or worshipping idols. To be considered as an apostate, one must have acted voluntarily and without coercion. Apostasy is grounds for the dissolution of marriage. Repentance, attested by two professions of faith, is enough, in the opinion of numerous jurisconsults, to lead to the dropping of the sanction.

For most doctrinal schools, *lex talionis* (*qisas*) is not part of the *hudud* and is dealt with separately. It is a personal injury for which redress is sought only at the request of the victim and the descendants of the victim. It concerns wilful offences against life or physical integrity, intentionality being measured by material and external criteria. In a case of murder, the closest relative of the victim can demand the execution of the murderer. In a case of physical violence, the victim or his relatives can request that an identical wound be inflicted on the person who committed the offence. Doctrine, however, encourages a recourse to conciliation, which consists generally of the payment of a blood price (*diya*), a monetary evaluation of the harm suffered by the victim. It is also applicable in the case of homicide or involuntary injury. Payment of the blood price restores the integrity of the person whose rights have been adversely affected. Offenders are, however, required to acquit their debts towards God by pious acts.

All offences that are not part of the *hudud*, *lex talionis*, and blood price are left to the discretionary judgement of the judge. Faced with these offences, a judge cannot pronounce a sanction which is greater than that foreseen by the *hudud*. In practice, discretionary judgement seems to have been more widely used. It can consist of corporal punishment, a compensatory fine, or public censure.

Based on the Sharia, *fiqh* constructed a complex and sophisticated structure made up of rules and precepts whose organization and logic are rooted in religious and moral as much as legal references. On the basis of refined epistemological categories, jurisconsults have identified and articulated the rules of a coherent normative system, capable of adapting, although in a conservative way, to the changing circumstances of Islamic societies. It is possible to have the erroneous impression that this system is a monolithic reality, but it is also true that with time it tended to congeal and lose its plasticity.

6

Practices and Institutions of Justice

The history of 'Islamic law' has, since the nineteenth century, made the theory–practice dichotomy its principal, even obsessive, object of study. For a long time it was said that doctrine (*fiqh*) was casuistry disconnected from reality, and that Islamic law was an abstraction distant from the practice of the *qadi*, the Muslim judge, often depicted as a symbol of arbitrariness. In a characteristic swing of the pendulum, it was then said that, far from being confined to the Platonic world of ideas, this doctrine had found the means of transforming itself into a system of law active in the social world, in such a way that one might talk of an Islamic legal system.

This oscillation is due to an academic tendency to raise questions without attaching them to a particular object of study or, at least, to postulate the existence of homogeneous models to which reality is made to conform, rather than accepting the plural and fragmented nature of the world, including that of norms and laws. As much as possible this chapter seeks to give an account of the institutions of this normativity and their functioning between the early Islamic period and the reforms instituted during the Ottoman Empire. One can note here that instead of a unified and homogeneous judicial structure, one can observe a variety of practices and institutions which rarely formed a system. It is not, from this point of view, aberrant to say that in societies where urbanization was a reality affecting a very small minority, local custom occupied a preponderant place, and that it was often only at a subsidiary level that Islamic doctrine and institutions could occupy a place of any consequence.

The concept of justice in Islam

Only a reifying and culturalist viewpoint makes it possible to talk of 'justice in Islam' or an 'Islamic conception of justice'. One has to recognize that theories and dogmas are nuanced, or even divergent. Beyond religious discourse, one has to acknowledge that justice is a practice whose contours enter with difficulty into a rigid framework. In the principal Islamic texts the terms associated with an idea of justice, understood broadly, are very numerous. They include 'right' (*haqq*), 'decree', 'judgment', 'equity', and 'justice' (*'adala*). This latter word and its derivatives figures in several Quranic verses, such as 'I have been commanded to be just towards you'[1] and 'Be equitable – that is nearer to godfearing.'[2] We can note that the Sunna is no less expansive on the theme of justice. One can quote the tradition according to which 'the most beloved of the creatures of God and the closest to him is a just imam'. With regard to the sovereign and judge, it is also said that 'when they judge they must be equitable' and 'he who is [a] judge must judge equitably'. It is noticeable also that the study of Tradition requires that the person who relates the deeds and statements of the Prophet should be just. This requirement has been extended to judges and witnesses in court.

The ninth and tenth centuries were marked, in the domain of theology, by the controversy between Mu'tazilites and Ash'arites, the followers of al-Ash'ari. The Mu'tazilites presented themselves as the proponents of justice and the oneness of God, and affirmed the primacy of reason in the determination of human acts. If the existence of the world presupposes an absolutely unique and transcendent Being Who is at the origin of the world, then humans must be assumed to act freely and be responsible for their acts. The Mu'tazilite conception of justice derives from this principle of the free will of humans. God, as the Just, cannot punish a person who is not responsible for his acts. He censures only an unjust act committed by an agent who intentionally does wrong. It is through reason that people can discover the good or bad nature of acts. In contrast to Mu'tazilite doctrine, Ash'arism constitutes itself as Sunni Islam's orthodoxy. The fundamental thesis is that human acts are predestined: humans do not desire anything themselves, their will is completely between the hands of God. If they are responsible, it is through 'acquisition' of their acts, not by their creation. God can do everything, including what humans may consider as evil and injustice, although intrinsically it is not, since evil is only offence against a norm and the Creator is not subject to anyone's norm. Justice, for al-Ash'ari, is 'doing what one has the right to do'; whatever the divine Norm proclaims to be just is just.

In the Platonic system of the tenth-century philosopher al-Farabi, the philosopher-king is entrusted with the mission of installing justice and bringing societies towards heavenly happiness, and religion only intervenes in order to federate human opinion and will. Another philosopher, Miskawayh (932–1030), sought, in the spirit of the *Nicomachean Ethics* of Aristotle, to develop a theory of the just mean. Averroes (1126–98), for his part, used reason to interpret revelation and, in return, legitimize philosophy on the basis of religion: God is always and necessarily just; humans exercise free will and are, therefore, responsible for their acts.

Treatises on governance form a genre which is characterized by a strong sense of pragmatism. Mawardi (972–1058) constructed a theory of caliphal absolutism tempered only by the dispositions of the divinely revealed Norm and the virtue required of the sovereign, who must be just. The same pragmatism led the scholar Ibn Taymiyya (1263–1328) to show how to restore the revealed Norm in the conduct of the affairs of the state which has the task of ensuring that justice is done. One can also note the existence of the treatises of *hisba*, founded on the Quranic injunction to command good and forbid evil (Quran III, 104).

The theme of Islamic justice continues to be the source of a significant volume of philosophical and political literature. This is particularly true in the field of economic and social ethics. Sayyid Qutb (1906–66), ideologue of the Muslim Brotherhood in the middle of the twentieth century, is thus the author of a work entitled *Social Justice in Islam*.

The institutions of justice

The question of justice is also understood in terms of the exercise of the power to judge. One must therefore consider the establishment and transformations of judicial power, not in the theories that have been proposed of such power, but in the historical forms it has assumed.

It is generally affirmed that the institutions of the early Islamic period and the norms they applied were in a certain sense contiguous with pre-Islamic practice. It has also been noted that Quranic notions such as *lex talionis* and blood price were to a large extent inspired by the Bedouin context in which the Quranic message was proclaimed. This context was marked by a strong tendency to regulate conflicts in a conciliatory rather than punitive fashion. This is doubtless due to the fact that the prevailing logic sought to maintain a fragile equilibrium between the various tribal formations rather than emanating from a centralizing and hierarchical political structure. Arbitration and the search for solutions founded on consensus were among the preferred forms of conflict regulation which, unsurprisingly, one finds in a number of contemporary contexts where social organization of a segmentary type prevails. A normativity operates which is founded on collective responsibility and honour.

With regard to responsibility, customary regulation is clearly distinguished from modern law. Whereas modern law is essentially articulated around the notion of individual will and responsibility, the regulation of conflict based on traditional customs makes the social group to which people belong the ultimate holder of rights and obligations. From this point of view there is no individual notion of 'person' – a legal concept we can note in passing. Customary regulation is established above all in a collective fashion and in a statutory manner within each community. Group responsibility is engaged by the acts committed by its members, on the one hand, while the rank of each member within the group is established in terms of his or her place in the social order, on the other.[3] The result, to give a schematic illustration, is that the wound inflicted on Ragab, a member of the tribe of Bani Hilal, by Laith of the Ait Marzuq tribe would make the Ait Marzuq responsible for paying reparation to Bani Hilal corresponding to the status that Ragab occupies in his tribe.

The arbitrator is a classic figure of the early Islamic period. It is recounted that a Christian poet, al-Akhtal, was called upon to arbitrate in a conflict between Muslims, inside a mosque. For his part the Prophet is reputed to have left Mecca at the request of Medinan tribes soliciting his arbitration. History has it that the Prophet and his successors, Commanders of the Faithful and caliphs, appointed judges in the different provinces of the empire. Thus the second caliph, 'Umar ibn al-Khattab, for example, appointed Abu Musa al-Ash'ari as judge of Kufa. The epistle declaring his appointment is considered by Tradition scholars as a model of judicial ethics. Historical research has contested the authenticity of this document, among other reasons because the earliest doctrinal works – those by Malik and Shafi'i – do not mention it, and it only appears at a later date, corresponding to certain attempts to institutionalize justice.[4]

It would seem that, from the earliest times, rulers sometimes appointed other judges, but these were ad hoc nominations. The constitution of the corpus of doctrine came later, and so their work was necessarily very personalized, a sort of 'melange of customary rule, governors' edicts and some general ideas of religious righteousness, according to the Quran and holy precedent'.[5] On this subject the philosopher al-Kindi recounts the anecdote of the Umayyad governor asking the Cairo judge one day: 'Do you have the Quran?' To which the judge replied: 'No!' The governor asked him: 'Do you know the rules for the division of heritage?' To which the judge again replied, 'No!' 'Do you know how to write?' the governor asked him then. 'No!' The governor again asked him: 'How can you pronounce a judgment in this case?' The judge replied: 'I judge according to what I know, and what I don't know, I ask.' The governor then patted him on the shoulder and said, 'On you go, you're a good judge!'[6] This stereotype of the ignorant judge, taking arbitrary decisions, is a constant theme in Islamic history.

Under the Abbasids, however, judicial functions were developed. The legitimacy of the Abbasid caliphate was entirely founded on its claim to embody religious piety and divine justice through fidelity to the Quran and Tradition. One could say that whereas the Umayyads claimed proximity to the Prophet through the agnatic line, the Abbasids advanced a claim based on their fidelity to his teaching. This was expressed through the reinforcement of the doctrinal schools, by the patronage of scholars, and the integration of some of them into the judicial structure. In addition, the judges of the large cities of the empire were increasingly appointed by the caliph. The fifth Abbasid caliph, Harun al-Rashid (763–809), was the first to appoint a 'judge of the judges', Abu Yusuf, as their head, thus adopting practices inherited from the Sassanid Empire.

It would be a mistake to believe that caliphal involvement in the delegation of the powers of justice corresponds to the construction of an organized judicial institution, systematic and centralized. One cannot apply a pyramidal conception of justice without committing a major anachronism. While the caliph formally appointed judges in major cities, the exercise of control over their activity was the responsibility of the governor. One should highlight that justice was a local matter and evaded every attempt at top-down structuring. The title 'judge of judges' should be understood as a court position rather than the charge of a ministry. In other contexts it was a title attached to a person rather than an administrative post with all that that implies in terms of powers of delegation.

The fragmentation of the Abbasid Empire and the break-up of the Islamic world were not without consequences for judicial practice. Local dynasties established their own judges, independently of Baghdad. The attribution of the function of judge – in the principal cities at least – reflected the scale of provincial autonomy in relation to the capital. Each rival caliphate put in place, in addition, its own judge of the judges, because this was an attribute of sovereignty. Under the Mamluks of Egypt a hierarchical structure of judicial power made its appearance, each province of the sultanate receiving a magistrate placed under the Cairo judge. This position was expanded subsequently with the appointment to the position of a 'judge of judges' in Cairo and then, in the main towns, of a judge belonging to each of the four main doctrinal schools. Their remit extended to routine justice, with the exception of the police, the market police (*hisba*), military justice, and legal decisions that were reserved for the sovereign.

It was under the Ottoman Empire that the administration of justice assumed, in an Islamic context, its most organized form. The judge (*qadi*) placed at the head of a court with jurisdiction over a given territory and installed in specific buildings, was competent in Sharia, the revealed Norm, and positive legislation (*qanun*). He was also empowered to impose discretionary sanctions. Appeals against the decisions of the judge were not expected, even though the imperial *diwan* could receive appeals and order a new judgment. The judges enjoyed immunity in that their work was in principle protected from interference by local authorities and they could only be judged by the imperial *diwan*. They could, however, be dismissed by the sultan at any time. Originally an appointment for life, it was progressively shortened, becoming only a year by the seventeenth century. This, together with the levying of unjust taxes, was considered one of the main causes of the later decline of the judicial system. The balance between Sharia, positive legislation, and civil, political, and military jurisdictions constantly varied. With the reforms initiated at the turn of the nineteenth century, a new law corpus and a new judicial system took shape. From this time onward, one can adequately call the traditional courts Sharia courts in the sense that their competence was henceforth limited solely to the domains of law directly inspired by the Sharia. The tendency to codify law, inspired first by religion and then in an increasingly secular tendency and the reform of the judicial system, continued to develop, resulting in the creation of secular courts with the birth of the Turkish Republic.

The judge between theory and practice

The nature of the work of the Muslim judge has animated many debates to the extent that the figure of the *qadi* administering justice in a casuistic and sometimes arbitrary way has become a sociological commonplace. Max Weber made him one of his ideal types in the domain of justice. This is echoed in legal anthropology, where one finds the affirmation that the judge in Islam is an intermediary whose task is to facilitate the return of parties in conflict to negotiation.[7] This conception is, however, decisively challenged by recent works of legal history which show that the accumulation by the Muslim judge of multiple functions in no sense means that his work is imprecise, erratic, or even arbitrary. Far from being a mere social intermediary, the judge, according to what one can discover of his work in the archives, seems trained in doctrine and in its application.

It is scarcely possible to draw a representative tableau of the function of adjudication in an Islamic context between the Prophetic period and the coming of the Ottoman Empire. The historical sources are too partial and the landscape is too fragmented. Generally two kinds of reconstruction are proposed: first, an idealization of the figure of the Muslim judge based on doctrinal sources which formalize the necessary conditions for the exercise of this function and the procedures to follow in order to exercise it correctly; and second, monographs that rely on archive resource from a specific place and time. The work of researchers such as Christian Mueller is of the second type. His research is concerned with specific archives – such as those of the Haram al-Sharif in Jerusalem, in Mamluk Palestine in the fourteenth century, and, on this basis, highlights the close relations that certain judges maintained with *fiqh*. The documents studied provide evidence of judicial practice guaranteeing the personal rights of the people for whom they were drafted. While past research concentrated principally on doctrinal works, manuals, and collections of fatwas, the study of documents relating to specific judicial practices shows how the activity of the courts was carried out in conformity with the procedural rules established by doctrine.

The Ottoman Empire, as we have seen, marks a turning point in judicial practice in an Islamic context. That also concerns the personnel in charge of dispensing justice. Judges were integrated into a hierarchy and career structure, at least in the highest spheres of power close to the official centre of gravity in Istanbul. Up until the period of Mehmet II it is difficult to speak in terms of a hierarchical corpus of trained individuals, but from the middle of the fourteenth century the rules of organization of the *'ulama* were codified, and defined the basis of a complex *cursus honorum* to which the final touches would be added at the beginning of the eighteenth century. This meant that the scholar of religious studies who wanted to attain a senior position had first to teach in a series of establishments ranked in a particular order before attaining a level that would make him eligible for high posts in the scholarly hierarchy. These posts were themselves ranked in order of importance.

Under the reign of Suleiman the Magnificent (1494–1566), also known as 'the Lawgiver', the function of the *mufti*, which hitherto had tended to be independent of the religious and administrative hierarchy, began to acquire a more institutionalized character. Thus the position of *shaykh al-islam* appeared, a post which was occupied concurrently with that of *mufti* of Istanbul. This official, veritable head of the *'ulama* and the principal religious authority of the empire, assumed the direction of a quasi-ecclesial institution which, 'with a resilient structure and hierarchy, linked to the state which provided it with financial support, was a phenomenon without equal in Islamic tradition'.[8] The sovereign expected that this dignitary and official, who remained apart from the *diwan*, would exercise control over orthodox belief and give a religious validation for the acts of the ruler. The importance of the responsibility entrusted to the *shaykh al-islam* gave him broad powers and, although the sovereign had in theory the power to appoint and dismiss the *shaykh al-islam* as he wished, in practice he remained dependent on the *shaykh*'s favour.

The age of reforms and the coming of the nation-state

Legal and judicial reforms continued in the Ottoman Empire until the Turkish Republic was set up. They concerned the status of magistrates – training, recruitment, salary – as well as the institutions themselves: new administrative and judicial jurisdictions, progressive separation of powers, the creation of a Ministry of Justice. One can observe the same reforming tendency across the countries of the Islamic world, whether they had been colonized or not.

The period of Muhammad 'Ali (1769–1849) marks a break in the history of the administrative and legal system of Egypt; 1818 saw the promulgation of the first official order defining the rules for the workings of administration. Administrative councils with judicial powers and instances were created, in parallel with the existing religious tribunals and consular jurisdictions. At this period certain questions could be dealt with by two parallel legal processes and lead to two different judgments, one pronounced by a Sharia judge and the other by a state official.

In 1875 mixed tribunals consisting of a court of first instance and an appeal court were established to settle disputes involving foreign subjects. The same model was followed in 1883, when native courts were founded with jurisdiction in cases involving Egyptian nationals, with the exception of matters relating to personal status. One can observe the same process in other countries. In Tunisia and Morocco reforms were initiated before the French protectorates were set up, in 1881 and 1912 respectively. In Algeria the colonial regime sought to dismantle the existing legal system in order to replace it almost entirely with a French system. The Anglo-Egyptian Condominium in Sudan was used to introduce elements of Egyptian justice in that country. Only the Arabian Peninsula remained apart from this general evolution.

All the judicial systems in Muslim-majority countries were profoundly transformed in the course of the nineteenth and twentieth centuries. Without correlating this transformation directly with colonialism, it is clear that law of religious inspiration was progressively restricted to the domain of personal status (marriage, divorce, affiliation, inheritance) and that the jurisdictions administering this law were gradually stripped of their powers in favour of more or less secular national jurisdictions. Iran, since the revolution of 1979, and Saudi Arabia, along with several Gulf countries to various degrees, constitute exceptions, even if this overall appreciation should be nuanced. Even in the 'reserved domain' of personal status, one notes the adoption of codified laws, a technique foreign to Islamic tradition, with application entrusted to specialized civil courts whose judges were trained in law faculties. From the 1970s onwards one can see a tendency to 'Islamization' of law judged to be too secular. This meant in practice the adoption of legislative texts that made explicit reference to the Sharia, which was often promoted to the rank of principal source of legislation (see Chapter 9).

In most countries in the Arab world, a judicial system similar to the French system was adopted. This is due partly to the colonial presence (Algeria, Lebanon, Morocco, Mauritania, Syria, Tunisia), but also to the existence of a tradition of legal cooperation marked by resistance to the British, as in Egypt. The Ottoman heritage and Egyptian influence in all the fields of law (Libya, Iraq, Gulf countries, Sudan) were also factors of importance.

While a certain homogeneity of Arab judicial experiences is perceptible, this gives way to diversity when one examines the Asian countries where Islam is the majority religion in demographic terms. From Turkey to Malaysia, and in Iran, Pakistan, Afghanistan, Bangladesh, and Indonesia, national experiences closely determine the form of systems for the administration of justice, whether it be secularism, federalism, or Islamic republicanism. The place given to Sharia can be non-existent, highly indirect, or, on the contrary, completely central, even if this centrality is more symbolic than effective. The judicial systems adapt themselves to these national particularisms.

To this general and contrasting survey one can add countries with a significant Muslim minority. This is the case in India, with one of the largest Muslim populations in the world; Thailand, where Muslims are increasingly affirming their presence; and China, where the regional and minority question, including the Muslim Xinjiang region, is highly sensitive. In all these cases the place accorded to the

Sharia is greatly dependent on the character of the state – pluralist or centralist and authoritarian – its recognition or not of the personal aspect of laws (particularly in family law), and its adherence to the great principles of human rights: freedom of conscience, freedom of worship, freedom of association. Judicial systems are not, however, marked by this minority presence except in the area of personal law, where states may have consented to the setting up of jurisdictions specifically for Muslims.

Sub-Saharan Africa presents a variety of different situations. The colonial heritage is one element, of course, with a marked contrast between the countries influenced by British Common Law and those whose law emerges from the Napoleonic Codes, countries whose federalism permits a wide degree of legal diversity and those with an essentially secular centralized system. As a consequence, Sharia sometimes is elevated to the status of substantive law and on other occasions is only indirectly present, as in Senegal. Each situation has a corresponding specific legal system, which is most of the time not influenced directly by Islamic normativity, except once again in the domain of personal status.

Justice has been much studied by Muslim scholars from philosophical and institutional viewpoints. Administration of justice has also been formalized. Its effective practice has been erratic according to 'place and time', to use the established expression in *fiqh*. Contact, whether colonial or otherwise, with the West, then, brought fundamental transformations in judicial organization and in the place occupied in emerging nation-states by Sharia and the jurisdictions that were based on it. We should now set about describing this transformation more closely.

7

The Invention of Islamic Law

What is called 'Islamic law' does not constitute an historical reality as old as Islam itself. The idea of transforming Islamic rules into law and, particularly, codified law is the result of an invention rooted in European intervention on the Muslim scene.[1] Orientalist scholars and colonial administrators, on the one hand, and Muslim rulers and the new elites, on the other, sought in Islamic norms and doctrine elements which could be moulded into positive law of a Napoleonic type. This process was successful, and the notion of Islamic law became part of political and legal thought both in Muslim-majority societies and where a strong Muslim minority affirmed its presence.

An administrative and academic creation

The study of Islamic law began in the West in the eighteenth and nineteenth centuries. A clear link existed between knowledge and power in so far as demand for knowledge of local law was driven by European expansion. At the end of the eighteenth century European powers, no longer limiting themselves to trading activity through posts established in foreign territory, began to establish colonies overseas, which meant administering the colonized peoples. To solidly establish their power and maintain the social order, European powers needed to know more about local norms, even if this meant imposing Western categories on questions which, *a priori*, were not formulated in such terms.

Towards the end of the eighteenth century, British linguists and jurisconsults were the first to consult local scholars on the rules governing Hindus and Muslims. Some decades later, French Arabists and soldiers carried out research in Algeria on the 'native laws' in force. During the same period Dutch scholars sought to understand which norms governed the life of the indigenous population in Indonesia. This research, of a practical nature, was centred on social features seen as legal in nature, and was linked to the broad project of incipient Orientalism: collecting, describing, and understanding the elements of other civilizations. This took place in parallel with the emergence of philological, historical, and ethnological studies as serious academic disciplines. Thus the studies of researchers from colonizing countries was part of a larger project of 'discovery' of Islam and Islamic law.

To answer these questions on 'local law' (often designated 'native' law), metropolitan and local researchers – who were often part of the colonial administration – used philosophical, historical, ethnographical, and legal approaches. From the beginning, the question of what law was and what it should be was discussed. Knowledge was not only a question of description and analysis, but also of normativity defined by Western legal positivism. The question of the relation between theory and practice, central in Western studies on Islamic law, finds its origin in these scholarly and political debates which began in the nineteenth century.

One example of the early intertwining of scientific and practical questions leads us to the Netherlands, where the colonization of Indonesia and above all Java and Sumatra had developed awareness of the theme of 'Islamic law'. After the departure of the British in 1814, the Dutch administrators knew very little about Islam and Islamic regulatory practices because they had not hitherto been involved in the administration of native communities. Policy evolved, however, with the emergence of the idea that a colonial government would be responsible for keeping order and administering justice by applying local norms. The Dutch government created institutions in Delft and Leiden tasked with training colonial administrators. In 1844 the Arabist Willem Meursinge (1832–60) published the first manual of Islamic law in the Netherlands. It was a sort of adaptation of a Malay manuscript in Arabic characters, written by a scholar from Aceh. This text was used as a manual to teach Islamic law to students of the colonial institute in Delft.

From then on, the learning of language (Malay and Arabic) and the study of Islam were closely linked in the training programme for colonial administrators.

Meursinge's successor, Salomo Keyzer (1823–68), had studied Hebrew and Judaic law before commencing law studies at Leiden, as well as the study of Arabic and Islam. Like his predecessor he never travelled to the Dutch East Indies. Primarily a philologist, he made a major contribution to the translation and commentary of the classical works of the Shafi'i school in Dutch and French, the scholarly language of the period. In 1853 he published an introduction to Islamic law, the first such work in Dutch, principally intended for his students in Delft. Keyzer underlined the importance of knowledge of 'pure Islam', which he opposed to the 'aberrations' of daily life in Indonesia. He even encouraged the study of Arabic by future colonial administrators. In his opinion, the law of the Indonesians was contained in *fiqh*, the doctrine of Muslim scholars whose texts Keyzer taught in their traditional order.

Colonial administrators stationed in Indonesia engaged in polemics with Keyzer. They believed that real law was rather to be found in the practices of the natives, and in their local customs, which were quite different from the norms stipulated by Islamic scholars and varied from place to place. From their point of view, the teaching destined for future colonial administrators should concentrate on customs, local interpretations, and native languages, instead of pure and universal Islamic law and classical Arabic. These polemics continued for decades. One of those involved in the controversy in the 1880s was the Arabist and scholar of Islam Christiaan Snouck Hurgronje (1857–1936). On his return to Leiden in 1906, Snouck Hurgronje imposed, in close collaboration with the jurisconsult Cornelis van Vollenhoven (1874–1933), the doctrine of *adatrecht*, Indonesian 'customary law', as an academic and administrative vulgate. These two scholars underlined the considerable difference between Islamic law as contained in the texts and local customs, and considered that the study of normative texts must be completed by fieldwork on native practices.

This doctrine acquired a canonical status with regard to the Muslim communities of Indonesia through the manual on Islamic law of Theodor Wilhelm Juynboll (1866–1948), in which the author systematically juxtaposed the classical norms of the Shafi'i school and the different local customs. This manual replaced previous works which had emphasized the orthodox doctrines of the Muslim scholars. For half a century all colonial administrators had to learn Juynboll's colonial vulgate by heart. This manual was the fundamental text in Dutch for the teaching of Islam and Islamic law.

The imposition of a positivist model

Differences between researchers on this topic meant that it was broadly and vaguely defined. The legal perspective nevertheless dominated. The conception of 'native laws' followed the evolution of the legal thought of continental Europe, and was influenced by national legislation and Napoleonic-style codification. Researchers had the responsibility of deciding whether a customary practice should be elevated to the level of a 'law'. This European vision of law meant that differences gave way to the imposition of the positivist model, which led to the introduction of new analytical categories, such as 'personal status', 'criminal law', 'public law', and 'private law', hitherto unknown to Muslim scholars.

Almost alone in the face of all other commentators, Snouck Hurgonje underlined the original character of Islamic normativity. *Fiqh*, which he considered a 'doctrine of duties' (*pflichtlehre*), was for him a deontology rather than a legal system. On the contrary, the use of the term 'Islamic law' implied a completely new conception of Islamic normativity, an 'invention'. This conception was foreign to the vision that Muslim scholars had of their own tradition, but it became dominant, to the extent that students were taught 'Islamic law' and 'Islamic legislation', and action was taken to introduce these two subjects into contemporary Islamic states.

Although the concept of Islamic law was invented by European scholars in the nineteenth century, they did not act alone. Their work was only possible because of the help of local collaborators, working on the sidelines but key actors in the collection of materials. It was not easy to collect *fiqh* texts. Often the role of informant was supplemented with other services: interpreter, translator, research assistant, and adviser. Some local collaborators worked for consulates as dragomans and combined their knowledge of Oriental languages with an expertise in prevailing norms. Later, colonial institutions were created specifically for the transmission of knowledge and the training of qualified personnel.

The Orientalist perspective, which transformed Islamic normativity into Islamic law, was taken on board by the collaborators from the 'Orient', because of their daily engagement with the colonial administration. They thus assimilated a new vision of their society and its mechanisms. Their scholarly production was less visible because they were not given the responsibility of composing the authoritative manuals and syntheses. They were more often assigned to the publication of texts, documents, letters, and copies of documents with a translation and lexicon, and to the composition of manuals of judicial practice and the translation of classical texts. With the passage of time an increasing number of these indigenous collaborators produced doctoral theses on the subject of Islamic law, in their native countries or in Europe. Some of them became famous, such as Pangeran Djajadiningrat (1886–1960), the first Indonesian to defend a thesis in the Netherlands, who became a statesman and professor at the national University of Jakarta, or the Egyptian 'Abd al-Razzaq al-Sanhuri (1885–

1971), a senior magistrate, professor, and author of several Arab civil codes.

These 'Oriental' collaborators were trained in law according to European norms, and their conception of Islamic normativity derived directly from this positivism. For them, the notion of 'Islamic law' was self-evident. Although belonging to local elites, these collaborators more often emerged from minority communities such as the Jews in North Africa or the Christians in the Near East, and were recruited as interpreters. Their marginal status made it both easier and necessary to enter into contact with foreigners. It was not only their careers that guaranteed them a livelihood and social promotion, but also a cultural transformation of the way in which they understood their own society as they explained it to foreigners. It was an 'Orientalism from the inside', so to speak.

A major innovation was the use of printed text instead of manuscripts, the traditional medium for works of *fiqh*. For centuries, Muslim scholars had opposed the printing of religious texts. After Napoleon's expedition to Egypt the situation changed, with written text essential for new forms of administration and teaching. Thus, text layout and organization changed in a radical way. With this new technology new ways of conceiving normativity were disseminated. In addition, whereas classical Arabic held pride of place in the science of *fiqh*, with sometimes a secondary place for local languages, the Orientalist study of

Islamic law gave a preponderant place to European languages. Local collaborators seeking advancement in the administration or in the academic sphere were obliged to express themselves in the language and concepts of Orientalist knowledge. Their work also had to be published by local publishing companies, and above all by editors in Europe if they wanted to make a name for themselves in the worlds of university and government.

A new way of conceiving Sharia

The Orientalist conception of Islamic law was guided by regional experiences of colonization. In each region researchers sought to 'discover' the specific configurations of customs and rules imposed by local notables: in Morocco the *'amal*; 'Kabyle law' in Algeria; Anglo-Muhammadan law in British India; and *adatrecht* in Indonesia. These regional understandings of Islamic law and its relation to custom were marked by different national understandings of governance and jurisprudence in each colonial *métropole*. Thus the image of Islamic law in the Maghreb reflected the French conception of positive law, civil-law positivism; while Anglo-Muhammadan law manifestly proceeded from Anglo-Saxon Common Law.

The reception of the positivist conception of law, which is illustrated by the promulgation of the *Mecelle* in the Ottoman Empire, continued to develop in the newly independent states. It still thrives, with codification initiatives multiplying from Iran to Indonesia. It is taught in law faculties, in Islamic countries and in Europe. From a legislative point of view, parliaments are today responsible for the adoption of these laws in Muslim-majority countries, although Islam and Sharia can form part of the rhetoric of debate. In judicial terms reference is almost always made to the founding sources of contemporary positive law: legislation and case law.

Reproduced across the generations in the West as in the East, this conception of Islamic law has continued to exist up until the twenty-first century. It has been naturalized, in a sense, in the eyes of researchers and Muslims themselves to such an extent that to speak today of 'the invention of Islamic law' can seem like sacrilege. In addition, the place given to Islamic law has evolved, although in an irregular fashion. On the one hand, Islamic law has occupied an ever more limited domain, in the sense that the substantive rules of law have progressively ceased to be derived from the corpus of *fiqh*. On the other hand, in the domains still officially regulated by Sharia, one can note a tendency to use new legal techniques such as codification or the procedures adopted by the examining judge. At first sight one might conclude that the changes are merely formal. This would, however, be a misreading of the effect that a change in economy and epistemology can have on the nature of the rules that are applied.

It is not in fact irrelevant that the identification of a legal regulation is the result either of a doctrinal and casuistic approach or of a legislative process. On these depend the modalities of revision of the norm, to name only one aspect. Nor is it unimportant that mechanisms of appeal against a judge's decision have been put in place and, going further, that appeals to a court of final appeal may allow an examination of legal principles: it is here that the epistemological shift reveals itself most clearly.

To all of the above elements is added a central phenomenon in the legal evolution of Islamic countries. Sharia and *fiqh*, in their classical form, may have largely disappeared, but law that refers to Islam, positive law which in terms of sources and reference is under the aegis of the Sharia, has emerged, and has broadly imposed itself. The immense majority of the constitutions of Islamic countries refer to Islamic law under one appellation or another. This requires an effort to conform not to any positive law code but to a moral norm. This is the reason for the growing importance of notions such as Islamic 'public order', in which legal technique occupies a secondary place to attempts to appreciate the socio-political atmosphere of the times.

Even in situations where Sharia finds itself 'again' projected into the heart of the legal system, this takes place according to institutional, procedural, and referential modalities partially or totally different from what they were before the nineteenth century. The return to the Sharia never consists of the utopian journey of which the supporters of authenticity and tradition dream, but is rather the imposition of a law that, despite claiming to be exclusively grounded in Islam, is nevertheless governed by the legal dynamics of a globalized world.

It is undoubtedly the case that contemporary experiences of the integration of the Sharia into the legal structure of nation-states has taken place in such a way that one can use terms such as upheaval, transformation of the general balance of Sharia, its fundamentals, and underlying sources and references. This is true at an institutional level with the setting up of constitutional structures which formalize the separation of powers, the hierarchy of jurisdictions, the legislative principle, popular representation, and the fundamental rights and freedoms. It is also true at the substantial level, as the applicable norms were broadly formulated by codification, which did not so much perpetuate *fiqh* in doctrinal terms as it avoided flagrant conflict with it.

8

Sharia in Contemporary Legal Systems

It has become difficult, when talking about law in Muslim-majority countries, to use the term 'Islamic law'. National designations – Indonesian, Iranian, Egyptian, Moroccan, for example – prevail. There is not in fact any transnational law common to all or some Muslims, independently of the citizenship that makes them part of the population of a state. The legal systems of individual states vary as a result of their own history. Thus in many countries with Muslim populations the colonial experience has left its mark, whether on the general legal framework or in the specific way that law refers to Islam. The adherence of different national legal systems to civil law or common law has also been a major influence. The accumulation of laws and the development of case law over several decades, or even over more than a century, have also been determining factors.[1]

Islamic normativity has been partly codified. This is what has been called 'Islamic law', and principally concerns family relations, a field where *fiqh* is most developed. The term used is 'personal status law'. Most countries with Muslim-majority populations have personal status codes drawing their inspiration, to varying extents, from the precepts of Islamic doctrine. *Fiqh* continues to exercise an influence in the area of *waqf*. In the area of obligations, contracts, and criminal law, the impact of *fiqh* is slighter, or non-existent, as each country's history is more specific in such legal areas. Religiously inspired provisions have sometimes been extended to new areas such as finance. These are usually contemporary developments in subjects little covered by *fiqh* but which find in the sacred text a justification for their regulation. The Quranic prohibition of usury could be an example. Finally, one can observe the phenomenon of constitutional referencing of the Sharia as a source of legislation.

Law takes form, in general and with regard to Islam in particular, partly in parliament chambers, but to an even greater degree in courtrooms, where judges apply laws to situations of conflict and enact legal dispositions that have the force of law. Judicial space is a special place in which Sharia, its role and influence can be observed, not only with regard to legal areas where Islamic doctrine continues to develop, but also to a series of other situations where Sharia is invoked not as the basis of rules for substantive law but as a source of moral inspiration in the interpretation of positive law.

Arab experiences under the influence of Napoleonic law

Most Arab countries have, in varying degrees, adopted legal systems inspired by the continental European model: a constitution sets out the institutional architecture of the state, and parliament is in charge of the adoption of laws.[2] The emergence of constitutional justice was a significant development at the end of the twentieth century. Legislative texts are therefore liable to be examined for their conformity to the dispositions of the constitution.

Under the influence of the Napoleonic model most Arab countries developed a system of positive law with the corresponding judicial institutions. This evolution took different directions, and depended on whether the adoption of the French model was indirect, as in Egypt, or due to colonial domination, as in the Maghreb or the Near East. In Egypt the development of a codified law and administrative and judicial reorganization go back to the period of Muhammad 'Ali and are part of the Ottoman context of the time. The move towards national and mixed legal codes and the setting up of competent jurisdictions to apply them heralded a reinforcement of the reform process and of the privileges granted to Westerners. The end of the Capitulations and the unification of the judicial system did not change the overall trend towards national, positive law. In the Maghreb the colonial influence was more direct, although one should distinguish the experience of each country. The French model was introduced on a wide scale, and this was not reversed by political independence. This does not mean that the law was mimetic or that there was not a specific evolution. In the Levant the colonial experience was shorter but the emergence of a class of polyglot Lebanese jurisconsults and civil law specialists ensured the continuation of the Western model.

The legacy of Napoleonic law has also influenced the place of Sharia, although in an uneven way. On the one hand, the proportion of Islamic law – the nineteenth-century creation discussed in the preceding chapter – was steadily reduced in the sense that the substantive legal rules were to an ever-lesser extent derived from the corpus of *fiqh*. On the other hand, there was a noticeable tendency in areas still covered by Sharia to adopt new legal techniques, for example with regard to codification, jurisprudence, or appeals.

Personal status law has long been presented, in the countries under discussion, as unaffected by the profound changes undergone by the systems of law and justice. This needs to be qualified, for several reasons. First, the difference between personal status and real status, as constituent parts of civil law, is quite specific to the Napoleonic system. Second, the legal elements of personal status have been widely codified, making them the product of the legislative work of the lawgiver and the interpretative work of the judge. Finally, the judges have above all been trained in positive law, to the extent that the search for applicable norms in classical sources of *fiqh* was often more difficult for them than a recourse to quasi-official compilations. One can therefore say that the proportion of Islamic norms was therefore reduced and aligned with the prevailing legal system. However, whether as source of the constitution (the Sharia as source of legislation) or as instrument of judicial regulation (Islamic public order), Islamic normativity was constantly present. This phenomenon does not reflect a direct line of descent from *fiqh* to positive law, but rather was the construction of a structure of identity with communal and national aspects, under the aegis of Sharia as a moral reference.

Beyond the Arab world, whatever the contrasts between individual situations, the evidence shows that a system of positive law has been developed and consolidated. Even when Islamic normativity has been given a central place, it has been according to modalities totally different from those of the pre-colonial period. The call for Sharia is never in reality a return to a Golden Age, but an interplay of references which absorb, inflect, and orient constraints and dynamics that operate on a global scale.

Personal status law

Often presented as the last bastion of Islamic law, personal status law (or family law) is an area where the influence of Islamic doctrine has persisted, and which has also longest resisted attempts at codification. That does not mean that personal status law has been unaffected by broad legal changes – far from it – but it is undoubtedly the sector where the structural principles and the main categories of *fiqh* have remained in use, starting with the criterion of identification of the law applicable to individuals: the religious confession to which they belong. Thus, with the exception of countries such as Turkey, where a strict system of *laïcité* has been imposed, in family matters the law that is applied is that of a person's religious community, with complex nuances.

In Egypt, personal status law has never been completely codified, but a series of texts inspired by Hanafi doctrine have been applied to it: the laws of 1920 and 1929, amended in 1985, on marriage and divorce; the laws of 1943, 1944, and 1946 on succession; the law of 2000 on questions of procedure and divorce. These texts constitute a common law intended to apply to all Egyptians, with the exception of situations resulting from marriages between Christians of the same denomination. In general, the various laws sought to strengthen legal protection for wives, albeit in a limited and indirect way. The laws of the 1920s were intended to give a framework for divorce and to facilitate divorce for women able to claim that their husbands had wronged them. In 1979 an attempt was made to restrict the contracting of polygamous marriages (presuming the moral harm undergone by the first wife), but the attempt failed. In 2000 a law introduced an important innovation, founded on the classical technique of *khul'*, allowing wives, for the first time in Egyptian legal history, to unilaterally obtain divorce – without agreement of their husbands or deliberation by a judge – as long as they gave up the material advantages derived from their marriages.

In Iran the coming of the Islamic Republic was accompanied, in family law, by a number of contradictory dynamics. Laws adopted under the old regime were mostly maintained, but with important amendments. The family protection law of 1975 was not abolished, but modifications were introduced. In 1984, for example, the penalties incurred for registering a polygamous marriage without the authorization of a judge were abolished. Temporary marriage was recognized by the Civil Code of 1935, although the law says nothing on how to register it. Laws passed after the revolution have tended to relax restrictions on polygamy and repudiation, but these changes have been offset by dispositions protecting women or giving them benefits. Thus a 1982 law on the marriage contract gave wives the right, under certain conditions, to half the couple's income after marriage. In the same way, a judge can give the right of divorce to a woman who requests it, if he considers that she has been adversely affected by her marriage. Since 1999 special family tribunals have operated. In the 2000s laws raising the minimum marriage age and increasing wives' rights to divorce and the custody of children have been promulgated.

In Indonesia the situation is different. While the state is not formally Islamic it grants, by a law of 1989, a particular status to religious tribunals, and in 1991 promulgated a law for the compilation of Islamic law. A code of 229 articles on marriage, inheritance, and charitable foundations has been elaborated and discussed by state jurisconsults and *'ulama*. In a particularly Indonesian fashion, this compilation does not function as a collection of dispositions that limit the capacity of judges, but as a guide which religious courts must 'as much as possible take into account'. There is an increasing tendency to use this compilation, although this has not prevented controversy around interconfessional marriage among other things.

In Morocco, in 2004 a new family code replaced the code elaborated after independence. The code is presented as the realization of the demands of civil society, thanks to the intervention of King Muhammad VI. The new *Mudawwana* is much longer and detailed than the code it replaces, and reformulates a number of dispositions and adds a series of new ones. Its last article specifies that for questions not dealt with in the *Mudawwana*, the prevailing opinions in the Maliki doctrinal school should have primacy. Among the major changes one can note the greater emphasis on the principle of equality between the spouses: both are invested with authority and have similar reciprocal duties towards one another. The wife is no longer required to be obedient to her husband. In addition, women can get married without the assistance of a guardian, and the age of marriage has been raised. The ban on Muslim woman marrying a non-Muslim remains in force, as does the obligation for a husband to offer a marriage gift to his wife. Polygamy is not abolished, but is put in a legal framework, and is limited in practice by the establishment of administrative conditions, including the agreement of the present wife, the prospective wife, and a judge. Repudiation is maintained as a principle, but is also submitted to the agreement of a judge, and has to meet several conditions such as the deposit of a sum of money guaranteeing the maintenance of the repudiated spouse and her children.

Criminal law and civil law

In most Islamic countries criminal law is no longer regulated by rules of Islamic inspiration. Some notable exceptions need to be mentioned. In Saudi Arabia, almost the only country not to have codified the essential elements of its legal system, criminal law is administered by judges relying on Hanbali doctrine, whose principal categories, detailed in Chapter 5, remain in force. In Pakistan, the law codes introduced by the British form the basis of criminal law, but they have been substantially amended by legislation aimed officially at Islamizing laws. It is in this way that amendments to the law on blasphemy have been made. Dispositions, claimed to be Islamic, concerning murder and assault have been incorporated into the penal code. And above all, in

1979, under the presidency of Zia-ul-Haq (1974–88), four ordinances on *hudud* were promulgated, concerning offences against property, fornication, false accusation of fornication, and the consumption of alcohol.

In Iran, a penal code was adopted in 1991. It consists of five books, one on the *hudud*, and contains, among other things, dispositions concerning banditry and 'earthly corruption' (*ifsad fi'l-ard*: violence directed against the essential human conditions for life), which have been used to repress political opposition. A recent project plans to abolish stoning for adultery, but introduces the crime of apostasy (*ridda*). Iranian penal law also lists a series of discretionary punishments and recognizes the principles of retaliation and the blood price. Finally, in 1991 Sudan adopted a penal code and code of penal procedure which defined six crimes as *hudud*: consumption of alcohol, fornication, false accusation of fornication, banditry, theft, and apostasy. The blood price and *lex talionis* have been also codified, in the same texts. Before the partition of the country in 2011, the Islamic 'penal code' was not applied in South Sudan.

Civil law has very largely moved out of the orbit of Islamic rules, which does not mean that explicit references to *fiqh* or Sharia cannot be found there. In Egypt the most important of these references is in the first article of the Civil Code, adopted in 1948, which stipulates the principle of the law's exclusive competence for all the subjects that it covers and, 'in case there is no applicable legislative disposition', the competence of a judge to adjudicate 'according to custom, and failing that, according to the principles of Sharia'.[3] Islamic normativity thus becomes the subsidiary source of legislation after law and custom. In the area of wills and succession an explicit place is accorded in this Code to Islamic Sharia and its principles, and it is also stipulated that it is forbidden for a Muslim woman to marry a non-Muslim.

In Iran a Civil Code was adopted under the Pahlavi monarchy in 1935 which, in the Napoleonic fashion, covers personal status. Although inspired by Shi'ite doctrine, this Code gave a secular and positive character to the Iranian legal system. It was secular in that courts were progressively handed over to judges outside religious hierarchy; positive because legal rules were detached from their origins in doctrine and submitted to the authority of jurisconsults trained in law faculties, and transformed into instruments of the authoritarian modernization policy of the ruler.

With the Islamic revolution, a movement calling for a 'return to the Sharia' was initiated, but never entailed the abolition of the inherited legal framework. The Civil Code, for example, was never abrogated, although around fifty of its articles were amended in 1982 and 1991. The work accomplished by the jurisconsults of the 'age of compromise and harmonization' around the 1930s enabled Iranian law to resist later ideological upheavals because Sharia was already at that time a material source which enriched positive law and did not prevent its development, but rather favoured its acceptance in society.[4]

The same process of secularization and codification affected Tunisian law. It has, since 1906, included a code of obligations and contracts which introduced important innovations with regard to the rules of Maliki and Hanbali *fiqh*. 'The innovations were all the more willingly accepted given that they responded to the imperative needs of modernization and development of the Tunisian economy through its alignment on the standards of the most developed countries, and thus those of the protectorate power [i.e. France].'[5]

Concerning Islamic banks

The first so-called Islamic banks were founded in Egypt in 1963. In the context of the increasingly emphatic affirmation of political Islam, and the generation of enormous capital by the oil boom, Islamic banks proposed a savings system which was not based on interest. As Saudi regional power developed, a particular reading of Islamic precepts imposed itself gradually. Most institutions and research on Islamic economics date from this period. At Lahore in 1974 the Organization of Islamic Cooperation founded the Islamic Development Bank, and in 1975 the first private Islamic bank was opened. In 1979, under the regime of Zia-ul-Haq, Pakistan Islamized its whole banking sector. The revolution in Iran led to a similar decision in 1983, while Sudan decided, even before the coup inspired by the Islamic movement of Hasan al-Turabi, to follow the same policy. There is a Dow Jones Islamic Market Index which follows the changes in the value of products and services according to the principles of Islamic finance. Citibank has opened Islamic branches and there are numerous financial institutions, in Muslim-majority countries as well as elsewhere (e.g. the United States and Europe), which today offer 'Islamic' products.

The justification for the search for a specifically Islamic form of financing is derived from the belief of Muslim jurisconsults that revenue is only considered legitimate if it is derived from a real sharing of the risks that have enabled it to be generated. In other words, usury (*riba*) is forbidden. This prohibition is founded on a Quranic text.[6] The notion of *riba* has also been the subject of controversy, with some observers concluding that it forbids excessive interest rates and others that the prohibition is aimed at at every form of fixed interest. These controversies continue. Two principal ways of interpreting these prescriptions have emerged at the present time. One involves a new interpretation in the light of the conditions of the modern world. The other sees itself as traditional, and calls for a literal interpretation of the corpus of rules of the Quran and Sunna. The approach of this latter tendency today dominates Islamic finance. Those articulating this approach find problematic the unshared aspect of risk and profit between lender and borrower. The principle of sharing losses and profits has produced an offer by Islamic financial institutions of a variety of products such as association, leasing, and limited companies.

Judges and Sharia

Legal practices are certainly more useful than the text of legislation in gauging the place of Islam and Sharia in contemporary law. A short typology helps us map these practices.

Firstly, situations in which judges seek to provide substance for references to Sharia (substantialization). An example is the situation regarding the wearing of the veil in public schools in Egypt, a question we examine below. In this case it is the definition of the Islamic norm that constitutes the object of dispute, with recourse to dispositions in positive law regarding religion, freedom of conscience, and worship. Decisions of the highest judicial instances, when they pronounce on the nature of Sharia as a legal reference, belong to this first category.

Secondly, situations in which Islam is used as the reason for decisions based on certain notions of public order (instrumentalization). In such cases, judges or other parties may use the concept of an offence against Islam as a means to accomplish other objectives. For example, the Moroccan Communist Party was banned in the 1950s, officially because it was offensive to Islam, but in effect as part of the struggle against the communist ideology.

Thirdly, the use of general principles, such as those of religion and the law derived from it, as a basis for decisions in a state that declares Islam as its official religion (over-determination). This invoking of general principles is often used in order to give extra weight to judges' decisions, in a stylistic formula which cannot be opposed. There are numerous situations in which a judge finds it useful to support the decision he has taken by a justification based on the canons of Sharia.

Finally, cases – very rare, however – where reference to Sharia is used to deny validity to positive law (invalidation). An example is the case of an Egyptian judge who, at the beginning of the 1980s, sentenced a person found drunk in public to flogging, contrary to the provisions of the country's secular laws. In this type of situation, a disciplinary sanction follows and the magistrate is removed from judicial duties.

An account of three court cases in Egypt which involved a recourse to the Sharia should provide examples that enable us to better assess how this principle might work, given the impossibility of being able to do this across the whole spectrum of Muslim contexts. The first case concerns the wearing of the veil in public schools. A father, as guardian of his two daughters, brought a case before the Administrative Court in Alexandria against the minister of education, requesting the suspension and cancellation of a decision that forbade the admission of his two daughters to secondary school. When he enrolled his daughters at a school he was notified that they had been excluded, on the basis of a ministerial decree forbidding pupils wearing the full veil (*niqab*) from entering school. The decree obliged pupils to wear full uniform, in conformity with regulations. The plaintiff considered that this contravened Articles 2 and 41 of the 1971 Egyptian Constitution.[7] The Administrative Court referred the case to the Supreme Constitutional Court. In its judgment of 18 May 1996 the Court underlined the freedom of the legislator to legislate provided that he respects the objectives of the Sharia. As the logic of the uniform was to ensure respect for girls' modesty and for social practices and customs, the Court considered that the legislator can legitimately impose limitations on dress, without this being contrary to the principle of protection of individual freedom, if the legislator's aim is to preserve identity. Islam, the judge added, had improved women's situation, which explains its insistence that they preserve their modesty. Islam ordered women to veil, as this constitutes a protection against vulgarity. With regard to dress, then, in view of the Law of God, a woman cannot exercise free choice. Her dress must, on the contrary, express the responsibility that she assumes in the world.

However, the configuration of female dress is not treated in an absolute and binding way by Quranic texts, leaving the way open to interpretation and intervention on the part of the legislator, who has to take into account morality as well as the necessities of life in a modern society. The Court concluded that the ministerial decree did not contravene article 2 of the Constitution. Establishing moreover a distinction between liberty of belief and liberty of religious practice, the Court emphasized that if the first of these liberties cannot be restricted the second can be limited by the pursuit of higher interests, such as public order and correct morality. Education is one of the higher interests that the state must protect and it authorizes the regulation of school uniforms. Consequently the Court dismissed the case. In practical terms this meant that the girls could not go back to school wearing the full veil.

The second case concerns the authorization of sex-change operations. This did not involve important legal developments, even though it generated much media attention. The case also was not situated explicitly on the terrain of Islamic law, while the conflict was essentially caused by divergent conceptions of morality inspired by Islam. In 1982 a medical student at al-Azhar University, Sayyid 'Abd Allah, consulted a psychologist, complaining of extreme depression. The psychologist examined him and concluded that the young man's sexual identity was perturbed. After three years of consultation she decided to send him to a surgeon, and Sayyid became Sally. This type of operation had numerous administrative and legal consequences. First, the dean of the Faculty of Medicine refused to allow Sayyid to sit examinations reserved for men, while refusing to transfer Sally to the Faculty of

Medicine reserved for women. To obtain this transfer Sayyid/Sally submitted a request to the civil registry office for a name change, which s/he was granted. Al-Azhar University, for its part, maintained that Sayyid, who had become Sally in the meantime, had committed a crime. The university considered that the doctor carrying out the operation had not changed Sayyid's sex, but rather had mutilated it, with the sole aim of allowing Sally to engage in homosexual relations. The representative of the Association of Doctors in Giza then summoned the two doctors who had carried out the operation to appear before a medical commission, which decided that they had committed a professional error by not confirming the existence of a pathology before operating. The Association wrote to the Mufti of the Republic asking for a fatwa on the question.

The fatwa concluded that if a doctor testified that the operation was the only remedy to the illness, the treatment was authorized. According to the Mufti, it could not only be the result of a person's desire to change sex, but must be the therapeutic result of a pathology diagnosed by the competent authorities. The fatwa seems to leave a margin of doubt as to whether the 'psychological hermaphroditism' from which Sayyid suffered could constitute an acceptable medical basis for the operation. Each party claimed justification for their position in this text. Al-Azhar took the case to court, on the pretext that the surgeon was liable to punishment because he had inflicted permanent damage on his patient. Applying the rules of criminal procedure, the public prosecutor began hearing the case and, as part of the process, consulted a medical expert. The expert came to the conclusion that if Sayyid was a man from a purely physical point of view, he was not from a psychological standpoint. The diagnosis of psychological hermaphroditism was therefore pertinent, and the surgical operation constituted an adequate treatment.

Alongside these controversial cases, family law is practised daily, in cases such as the fairly common one of a woman asking a judge to grant her a divorce from her husband because of the harm he has inflicted on her: assault, insults, abandonment. In his decision the judge first carefully documents the facts, the legal basis of divorce in cases where harm is done, the jurisprudential definition of prejudice ('the wrong committed by the husband against his spouse through violence, insults, or abandonment of the wife by her husband'), the criteria for the establishment of prejudice ('that which renders the continuation of married life impossible'), and its establishment by evidence given by two men or one man and two women. On this basis the judge can pronounce an irrevocable legal divorce on grounds of prejudice. This judgment shows us how a legislative rule (judicial divorce because of prejudice) is interpreted and put into practice by an Egyptian judge. He acts in a formal context which he has to respect. At this level it is clear that he orients himself to the technical aspects of procedural law. This can include references to dispositions explicitly linked to Hanafi law concerning witnesses, for example, but that takes place through the jurisprudence of the Court of Cassation. In addition, judges must have recourse to common sense in order to determine whether the matter brought before them belongs to a legal category, and if so, to which one. Overall, then, even when reference is made to Islamic law, it plays only an indirect role, through positive law and its institutions, and via the medium of judges, who reason as people of their time rather than as technicians of *fiqh*.

Experiences in incorporating Sharia are contradictory, and are evidence of an upheaval of equilibria prevailing in the legal field, including the presence on the scene of the state, positive law, and the human legislators who make law. With a few rare exceptions Sharia is no longer directly applied. In certain areas, certainly, one can establish a relationship between Sharia and the law in force, but a single tree must not obscure the forest. In parallel, new forms of reference to Islam and Sharia have appeared. Rather than a decline in references to Sharia, we can thus observe its radical transformation.

9

The Sharia

Political Uses and Constitutional Renderings

Contemporary experiences of integrating Sharia into the legal framework of independent states have taken place in such a way that one can speak in terms of an upheaval affecting the economy and epistemology of Islamic normativity. Its general equilibrium, fundamentals, and morphology – what one might also term its grammar – have been completely transformed. This is true with regard to the substance of the law, with applicable norms being largely formulated in a codified form. This was the subject of the previous chapter. It is also true from an institutional point of view, with the putting in place of constitutional structures which formalize the separation of powers, the hierarchy of jurisdictions, the legislative principle, popular representation, and basic rights and freedoms. The Sharia becomes the bearer of a frame of reference rather than specific rules which can be directly applied.

The recourse to a particular type of terminology does not necessarily mean that the same language is being spoken. One can observe the use of Sharia vocabulary in various contexts without there being a high degree of permeability between the argumentative logic of these different language repertoires. This is not due to different levels of truth but to the aims of the people involved in these discursive activities. As law, Sharia is a nineteenth-century invention; as a reference in political language, it is a formulation dating from the second half of the twentieth century; as a constitutionalized source of legislation, it is an innovation of the last quarter of the twentieth century; and as an ethical paradigm separate from legal normativity, it is a contemporary revival.

Sharia has imploded, leading to disassociation between legal and ethical normativity.[1] Each of the two domains is henceforth autonomous at least in appearance, according to very particular modalities. In the middle of the twentieth century reference to Islam was confined to the margins of political, ethical, or legal discourse. Then, under the pressure of national, regional, and international dynamics, it began to gain influence, at a grass-roots level – what one might call the re-Islamization of society – as well as from the top down, with Sharia elevated to the level of a political and constitutional reference point. This dynamic is more nuanced than it seems: the arrival of Islamo-conservative governments does not necessarily mean that Sharia-centred political and constitutional systems were put in place.

Implosion, eclipse, return to the political scene

In the twenty-first century what is commonly called Sharia concerns above all morality. The tensions observable in the political and constitutional domains derive from the complex relationship in modern societies between politics, religion, law, and morality. In a context of political emergence of the nation-state and the adoption of legal codes, a phenomenon one can find even in Meiji-era Japan, Sharia was pulled in different directions by the tendency of each of its elements to become autonomous. The end of the nineteenth century in Egypt, for example, saw the demarcation of a public sphere, a dynamic involving the codification of law and the emergence of a constitutional movement. This reconfiguration brought with it a state apparatus and means to legally regulate relations between state and citizens. It led to the progressive fragmentation of Sharia between a legal domain, where it acquired a circumscribed and positive legal character, and a public domain, where it acquired hegemony as a point of reference articulated around a nucleus presented as authentic, civilizing, and normative.

The ambivalence of Sharia is reflected in the different conceptions held by those who affirm their adherence to it.[2] It can sometimes be 'the basis for the law', on other occasions 'a life project', or something else entirely: 'Islam is not and never can be simply a collection of legislations', said an Egyptian attorney in the 1990s. Thus, in a general way, Sharia is a point of reference, not a precise set of contents, evoking an authentic tradition which society believes to be the only source of legitimacy. What this reference achieves varies according to the protagonists' variegated worldviews.

Pan-Arabism was originally only a variant of nineteenth-century nationalisms. The idea of Arabism was centred on the notion of the Arab caliphate. Arabism and an affirmation of Islam were articulated together. This tendency can be identified even in the doctrine of the Ba'th, the quintessential Arab nationalist party: 'Islam is the vital impulse which revealed to the Arabs the strength within them and projected them onto the stage of history.'[3] Although less doctrinaire, Nasser's discourse is marked by similar characteristics, which reveals that the opposition between Nasser and the Muslim Brotherhood was not related to ideology as much as to the struggle for power.

Algerian socialism was not without references to Islam, or even an early form of Islamism. The Association of Algerian Muslim 'Ulama, founded in 1931, was in a strong position at the time of independence in 1962. Its influence manifested itself in the elaboration of the doctrine of Islamic socialism. The early 1970s were marked by a strengthening of the Islamic tone of official discourse and the launching of the review *al-Asala* (Authenticity), which expressed the ambivalent nature of Algerian Islamism both within the state and outside it. The review symbolized how Islam was used by those in power as well as the fundamentalist project of a group among the Algerian elite. This Islamic theme expressed itself most strongly – without ever fully achieving its aims – in the Arabization policy and the adoption of the Personal Status Code.

It is therefore false to claim that Islam as a reference disappeared during the first three quarters of the twentieth century. It was nevertheless subordinated to the primordial aim of creating nation-states, expressed in constitutions as 'realizing the unified Arab state' (article 1 of the Iraqi Constitution of 1970) but also the primacy of the 'defence, consolidation, and preservation of Socialist achievements' (article 59 of the Egyptian Constitution of 1971). In the Arab context, the failure of nationalism, the 1967 defeat, the lack of freedom, and the impossibility of successfully implementing authoritarian modernization policies were all factors that facilitated the emergence of an Islamic political vision. The first part of the twentieth century was marked by the replacement of the idea of the utopian caliphate with the idealized Arab nation, while the second part of the century was characterized, among the Islamists, by a hoped-for return towards the original founding utopia of Islam. This would be made possible by the inability of nationalist culture to compete with religion and consequently to permit the development of ideologies that could be a counterweight to religion.

At the same time, religion's return to the foreground as a founding reference was broadly supported by the Arab regimes, which had little difficulty in exploiting the points of ideological convergence. The unitary utopia was one of these. Certain Islamic movements did not hesitate to use the term *ba'th islami* (Islamic resurrection), while nationalists appropriated the term *umma* (community), adding to it the term 'Arab' in parallel to the *umma islamiyya*, the Islamic community to which all religious literature refers. The notion of social justice is another of these points of convergence. Evidence of this can be found in the writing of Sayyid Qutb (1906–66), the Iranian revolution's rhetoric of the deprived, or the socialist discourse of most of the Arab states in the 1960s.

The multiple convergences between nationalism and Islamism enable us to understand the extent to which the nationalist project never sought to distinguish itself from the Islamic grounding of societies, but rather attempted to find Islamic roots which justified its plans, while marginalizing the original proponents of 'the return to the sources'. The stumbling block was not therefore principally ideological; the stakes were more political in character. The ingredients of Islamism include the denunciation of the illegitimate holders of political power, the contestation of authoritarian practices, and the combating of nepotism and corruption. The challenge was all the greater for the regimes in place because secular forms of opposition had failed, or had been taken over by the authorities. Governments reacted in various ways: making concessions (Egypt), using violence and intimidation (Syria), or Islamizing the state (Sudan), a technique which aims to give the regime a stability that coercion alone is not able to provide, to confer on it a legitimacy that makes the Islamists' claims ineffective.

There is therefore a double convergence between nationalism and Islamism, on the one hand, and the appropriation and manipulation of Islamic rhetoric by the regimes in power, on the other. This explains why the victory of the Islamic political groupings following the inaccurately named Arab Spring was not accompanied by a massive recourse to the vocabulary of Islam and the Sharia. The re-entry onto the scene of opposition parties rooted in political Islam is unsurprising when one remembers that the only organized groups opposed to authoritarian regimes had moved away from Marxism and socialism towards religious authenticity. At the same time, in Islamic terms, little distinguished the regimes from their opponents. In Egypt, the bigwigs of the National Democratic Party – the majority party led by Hosni Mubarak and later his son Gamal – tried to outdo one another beneath the dome of the parliament building in showing off their piety. In Algeria several parties calling themselves Islamist have been part of the government for years, a government that has embarked on the construction of the largest mosque in the world. Sudan has adopted a penal code with an Islamic 'label'. It is difficult to outdo the Saudi monarchy in terms of dogmatism. Overall, a requirement to be relevant in Islamic terms has long imposed itself in public space – indeed, it has become inescapable. It is impossible not to acknowledge this necessary relevance. It has also become obligatory to engage in a process of inflation of references to Islam, as soon as the first steps in this direction have been taken. In this respect one can say that ideological Islam has been subsumed in political Islam – that is to say, in the manoeuvres of power and politics.

Indispensable reference, diversified content

Reference to the Sharia can take different forms, of which some are political. This can be in an institutional context, in an electoral process, or in demonstrations of opposition to political authority. These political uses of Sharia are enacted on the basis of a repertory of terms of a religious nature which confers credibility on action carried out in its name. That does not mean that religion and politics are mixed together; on the contrary, each of them obeys multiple logics which sometimes converge. Nor does it mean that political uses of religion are merely cynical, any more than it excludes the calculation of costs and benefits. When politicians call, in the name of religion and personal conviction, for a law to prohibit the sale of alcohol, they do not only act under the influence of their desire to see the divine Norm applied. They formulate a political position that is favourable to them because it corresponds, according to their evaluation of the situation, to one of the expectations of public opinion. They can therefore with complete confidence anticipate a boost in popularity or an electoral gain. At the same time, such a calculation is only possible if the system of reference on which their suggestion is based is a credible one, which means, in the Islamic context, if the game of religious language is broadly present on the scene, disseminated, and accepted.

One can see that the reference to religion has origins beyond politics to which it cannot be reduced, although it does influence politics directly. The fact that people may act on the basis of political calculation is not in contradiction with the fact that they are convinced that their demands are right. One can at the same time desire power, fight for a norm, and seek to accede to power by using a religious norm.[4] From this point of view, the political uses of the divine Norm do not form an Islamic conception of politics, but a normal way of acting politically through the use of an Islamic frame of reference. This functions in a routine fashion, since it consists of relating a position to principles which are generally recognized and thus taken for granted. As what is automatically accepted does not require to be proved, this favours a limited form of argumentation and obliges other protagonists to align their own discourse in a similar way. It is not easy to contest in public what is widely recognized. That does not at all mean that there is general agreement on the content given to this common repertory of references. What people understand by a reference point such as Sharia can vary widely, and the consequences they draw from the use of this widely accepted reference can be different, and even contradictory. Particular circumstances give a specific content to the term 'Sharia', which takes a particular form according to the situations in which it is invoked. It is not possible to know in advance, with certainty, what arguments will be advanced, and which will be decisive, on subjects as varied as, for example, loans with interest, divorce on the initiative of the wife, biomedical ethics, reconstruction of virginity, homosexuality, the sale of alcohol, tourism, the wearing of the veil, apostasy, or blasphemy.

This content is not invented in an opportunistic manner by cynical political actors, but there is an extremely wide range of possible solutions from the point of view of the Islamic norm that serves as a reference. A political balance of power, based on a moral vision of the world, is what leads to one particular configuration prevailing over another. In other words, what varies is not the content of Sharia, but the state of opinion about what constitutes this content. 'From this point of view, relying on the divine Norm in the course of political action, is first of all to rely on a state of opinion – at least as it is interpreted. This is of course an eminently political attitude. Politicians generally act in this way. Moreover, nothing is more normal, since it is the course and the variations of this opinion that determine at least partially their destiny, or, more bluntly, the course of their career.'[5]

These political manoeuvres involve, above all, conformism, which a political actor can only with difficulty avoid without paying a heavy price. In societies with a Muslim majority, conformism entails referring in a conservative way to Islam and its norm, the Sharia. Each politician can appropriate the Sharia for his own ends, but that presupposes accepting the obligation to recognize the primacy of Sharia, even if symbolic, as a condition of political activity in a Muslim context.

Legal references to Islam and devolution of powers in religious subjects

The expression 'Islamic law' has become inaccurate as a way to designate the law of Muslim-majority countries and a series of mechanisms, which are not part of the continuity of *fiqh* but are among the techniques associated with contemporary lawmaking and constitutionalism. One can observe a particular phenomenon, in, *inter alia*, the constitutions of Muslim-majority states. This is the referencing of Islam, the Sharia, and *fiqh*. It is no longer a question of codifying Islamic law, but, essentially, of referring contemporary lawmakers to it so that it inspires their work. This applies to provisions that make Islam the state religion, stipulate that the head of state must be a Muslim, or make Islamic normativity the source of inspiration for positive law.

With the transition movement initiated by the overthrow of the Tunisian regime in January 2011 and the preparation of new constitutional texts, this question acquired new relevance, all the more so as conservative Islamic parties emerged victorious from the elections. The concern for political consensus seems to have prevailed over the desire for religious hegemony and ideological pragmatism over the utopian ideal. One of the reasons why this pragmatic tendency has prevailed so easily is most probably located in the plasticity of the Sharia and its capacity to function as a flexible resource rather than as a set of constraining rules.

Many constitutions of Muslim-majority countries refer to Islam. This is usually in four areas: the preamble; the designation of a state religion; the principle of the conformity of legislation to the tenets of religion; and the conditions that the head of state must meet. Designating Islam as a state religion is an old practice, going back to the 1950s.[6] Certain constitutions reserve the high offices of state to Muslims and the succession to the throne through Muslim offspring. Several constitutions also limit certain rights and freedoms in the light of Sharia, while affirming the central character of the family formed around religion and Islamic values. Most fundamental texts have consecrated the normative value of Sharia, principles of Sharia, and Islamic *fiqh*, but diverge on the place that should be given to this normative value. Three specific constitutional experiences allow us to observe the contrasting nature of references to Islam.

In Egypt, the Constitution of 11 September 1971 marks a break in that it introduces, for the first time, a reference to the normativity of Islam in the institutional system. Article 2 states that 'the principles of Sharia are a principal source of legislation'. On 22 May 1980 article 2 was amended to state that from then on 'the principles of Sharia are the main source of legislation'. For the special commission tasked with preparing the reform of the constitution, this new formulation aims at 'obliging the legislator to have recourse to the commandments of Sharia, to the exclusion of any other source, to discover in them what he is seeking; if then legislators do not find an explicit instruction in the Sharia, they can, through deduction from the sources of interpretation of the Sharia, determine the rules that one should follow.'

On the basis of this article, numerous constitutional challenges have been brought before the Supreme Constitutional Court (SCC) whose precedents are of particular interest. Initially, this jurisdiction tended, when a constitutional challenge was brought before it, to avoid venturing on to the terrain of interpretation of Sharia. Thus on 24 May 1985 the SCC cancelled the Jihan legislative decree, named after the wife of President Anwar al-Sadat, who inspired it.[7] This decree sought to reform the personal status provisions, and it was cancelled, not because of its purported contravention of article 2 in its newly amended form, but for the purely technical reason that the legislative decree, part of the special powers conferred by the Constitution on the president of the Republic, should not be used to change a text dating from 1929 and unmodified since then. In another decision issued on the same day the SCC formulated a principle which became a legal precedent. The basis of the legal action was that the Ministry of Waqf and the medical faculty of al-Azhar had been ordered to pay a sizeable debt, to which interest was added, as the Civil Code stipulated. This article of the Civil Code was the object of a constitutional challenge, and the SCC then laid down the principle of the non-retroactivity of article 2. 'The obligation imposed on the legislator to take the principles of the Sharia as principal source for legislation … only applied to legal texts promulgated after the date on which this obligation came into force. … As for laws preceding this date, they cannot for this sole reason be subject to this obligation and are therefore outside the scope of the constitutional review.' The Court added that the application of Sharia as though it were a collection of codified rules would entail a risk of contradiction and the destabilization of legal order.

However, with the passage of time, the possibilities for constitutional challenges concerning texts dating from after the 1980 reform multiplied. In a decision of 15 May 1993 the Court situated itself explicitly in the domain of Sharia and its interpretation. In this decision the Court detailed what should be understood as Sharia and what, in this context, could be the object of a process of interpretation. The question was that of a divorced woman who had brought an action in order to obtain the custody of her son and the right to remain with him in the former marital home in conformity with Law 100 of 1985. She also claimed the right to receive compensation of an amount equivalent to ten years of alimony payments. Her ex-husband had brought a case before the court, arguing that these two provisions were not in conformity with the Sharia. In its decision, the Court established a distinction between absolute Islamic principles and relative regulations. For the Court, the only principles to be applied without a margin of interpretation are those 'whose origin and signification are absolute' – that is to say, the principles that represent undisputed Islamic norms, whether from the point of view of their source (Quran, Sunna, consensus, analogy) or their signification. There exists, however, in the opinion of the SCC, a collection of rules considered to be relative, subject to interpretation, evolving in space and time, that are susceptible to divergent interpretations and can adapt to the changing needs of society. If the SCC 'recognized the legal value of the principles of the Islamic Sharia and the necessity for the legislator to respect "principles whose origin and signification are absolute", it was paradoxically to limit the effects of these principles. The Court is constrained by the norms which emerged from Islamic Sharia, but reserves itself the right to determine the content of these norms.'[8]

A new Constitution was promulgated in Egypt on 26 December 2012. It included article 2, while adding a new provision, article 219, which established that the 'principles of the Islamic Sharia include its general proofs and its fundamental and doctrinal rules, as well as its sources taken into consideration by the schools of the People of Tradition and Consensus'. The convoluted formulation of this article and its insertion at the end of the text are evidence of the rushed character of the adoption of the Egyptian Constitution, but they also reflect the will to circumscribe the powers of the SCC, by defining, on its behalf, the term 'principles of the Sharia' formulated in article 2 of the Constitution. The coup of July 2013 led to a resumption of work on the Constitution. The new regime, which removed the Muslim Brotherhood from power, gave a commission of experts the task of proposing modifications to the 2012 text. Another Constitution was drafted by this commission which integrated article 2 but removed article 219. It was approved in a referendum in January 2014.

Unlike Egypt, no text in Tunisia makes the Sharia a formal source of law. In the 1959 Constitution the first article stipulates that 'Tunisia is a free, independent, and sovereign state; its religion is Islam, its language is Arabic and its system of government is the republic'. This formulation was adopted on the initiative of the former president, Habib Bourguiba, in order to overcome the differences that had appeared in the first Constituent Assembly, although it was dominated by the members of the National Front, composed of the Neo-Destour and its allies. This formulation, along with the preamble which invokes Islam, ensured that there were interstices, which conservative – often Youssefist – elements on the fringes of the judicial authorities rushed to occupy.[9]

Tunisian judges have in part used the article to give Sharia the quality of a subsidiary source, in case of lacunae or obscurity in the law, particularly in the domain of personal status. In legal decisions relating to this, Sharia constitutes the 'source' of the personal status law, while in theory it is only one source among others. In other branches of civil law certain judges have also had recourse to Sharia, citing the fact that it has constituted one of the material sources of the code of obligations and contracts. Tunisian legal doctrine has long questioned the right of a judge to raise Sharia to the rank of a subsidiary source. For those in favour, the question was to know which was the good interpretation of the Sharia while for those opposed, the question was to imagine by what means the Sharia could be excluded from the positive legal system.[10]

These tensions appeared again at the time of the political transition initiated by the fall of the Ben Ali regime. The question of using Islam and Sharia as a reference has been the subject of animated debates. A paradox has developed: on the one hand, the political scene is polarized around the opposition between Islamists and liberals, whereas on the other, the presence of Islamic references in official texts is limited. Under the pressure of the opposition as much as its own political pragmatism, Ennahda, traditional representative of the Islamo-conservative tendency and leader since 2011 of the government produced by the country's first free elections, gave up the idea of making the Sharia a source of legislation. This does not mean, however, that Ennahda has abandoned its project of basing both society and state on Islamic values, although Rashid al-Ghannushi declared in 2016 that the role of the party had become strictly political.

After many twists and turns a new Constitution was adopted in January 2014. Article 1 stipulates that 'Tunisia is a free, independent, and sovereign state, Islam is its religion, Arabic is its language, and the system of government is the republic'. Furthermore, article 6 declares that 'the state is the guardian of religion. It guarantees freedom of conscience and belief, the free exercise of religious practices and the neutrality of mosques and places of worship from all partisan instrumentalization. The state undertakes to disseminate the values of moderation and tolerance and the protection of the sacred, and the prohibition of all violations thereof. It undertakes equally to forbid accusations of apostasy and the incitement of violence and hatred, and to block such incitement.' Sharia does not have a role in the Tunisian constitution as a legislative reference, as in Egypt, but this does not prevent Islam from being used as a resource, given that it is the religion of a state that is required to ensure that the sphere of the sacred is respected. The political climate will determine the interpretation of provisions about which there is no consensus. The notions of 'Islam' and 'Sharia' contribute to the structuring of the political sphere, while retaining a strong element of plasticity. These notions have survived various upheavals, and their longevity is evidence of a certain ideological permanence. What has changed are the rules of political practice and, among other things, the introduction of electoral competition.

The case of Morocco is equally interesting, with regard to the question of Islam as a source and the devolving of religious competences. The 2011 Constitution is situated within the continuation of a reformist evolution which had been accelerated by the Moroccan version of the Arab Spring, used by the authorities as an opportunity to embark on a process of consensus-based remodelling of the political sphere. With regard to the place of religion, one can notice the distinction between reference to Islam and the devolving of religious authority. Contrary to most constitutions of Arab League states, Islam is mentioned in a rather laconic fashion. Article 3 declares that it is the 'state religion' while recognizing 'freedom of worship'. Although freedom of conscience is not recognized in the Constitution – despite its presence in a previous version – article 25 stipulates that 'all forms of the freedoms of thought, opinion, and expression are guaranteed'. Contrary to the technique of restricting the scope of the stipulation by referral to the law – which limits the application of the stipulation or imposes conditions on its application – this text establishes an intangible principle. One can thus see that the pre-eminence of Islam is not accompanied by a reference to Sharia or *fiqh*. Islam, the state religion, is above all a reference with a national dimension. The text specifies that in its 'moderate version, the "Muslim religion" constitutes one of the unifying elements of the State, with national unity, territorial integrity, and the one and indivisible identity of the Nation' (article 1). The articles of the Constitution that refer to Islam almost systematically foreground the principles of tolerance and openness, as well as freedom of worship. A characteristic of the Moroccan constitutional system is, unlike situations where the religious legitimacy of the head of state is absent, the superfluous character of the identification of Islamic normativity as a constitutional referent.

The new Constitution is distinguished from preceding texts by its dissociation of the duties of the king as head of state and supreme arbitrator from those as Commander of the Faithful (*amir al-mu'minin*). It is also distinctive by the care it takes to reduce the possibility of transferring the competences of the head of state to the Commander of the Faithful. The Moroccan system is unique in that it is capable of limiting the normative field of Sharia in a measure which is inversely proportional to the centrality of the king as Commander of the Faithful. Where, as in Morocco, the symbolism of the king as Commander of the Faithful is a strong one, the normativity of the Sharia is less of a determining factor in political terms, 'as if the strength of the role of Commander of the Faithful has a compensatory effect for the weakness of the normativity of Sharia'.[11] Morocco is therefore a case of over-assertion of the monarchical order rather than of Sharia. The power of the king reinforces or goes against the normativity of Sharia depending on whether he wants to use it to his advantage or, on the contrary, contain it. When the aim is to give a national colouration to the legal order by Islamizing its sources, or to keep leftist political movements in check, the tendency is to exploit Sharia in an opportunistic manner. However, when the advance of Islamic parties is to be halted, the tendency is to restrict Sharia's normative role by relying on the Islamic concept of the Commander of the Faithful.

The Sharia as ideology

No matter how destabilizing a proposition it may be for those attached to permanence, we know that religions change. This is true of Islam, which is not a 'nomocracy' irrevocably trapped in its past. The way in which the religious and political domains are articulated together has a direct effect on the form of the discourses used to legitimize authority. Such discourses veer between ideology and utopia. Just as it is difficult to extract a political, constitutional, or moral truth from the sources of Islamic normativity, so too it is clear that people, when they refer to a foundational past and interpret it, take part in the re-creation of their tradition. In so doing, they create utopias. When these utopias are grounded in political and social reality, they need to be transformed into ideologies in order to be realized. It is not far-fetched to think that this function of Sharia is today reinforced, particularly in the context of the accession to power of Islamo-conservative parties.

Political ideas, as they take shape, rely on what makes sense in a particular context, in a movement of re-appropriation which allows them to assume the weight of normativity while retaining a degree of freedom in giving this normativity a new content. From this process of ideological sedimentation new rationalizations emerge. Political discourse claims to express – while in fact it constructs – what everyone is expected to know, producing a feeling of belonging, continuity, and coherence. Whatever its degree of innovation, ideological discourse incessantly reaffirms its connection to pre-existing, deep links to the past which enable it to project a highly personal version of reality into the world of public consensus, and at the same time to present its authority as being natural.

Islamic normativity is being integrated into the political and constitutional spheres, as well as the moral and social spheres in general. Sharia, in so far as it associates a way of understanding the world with a system of values, and is imagined in this way, tends to be particularly exploitable in ideological terms. Sharia, in the context of Muslim-majority societies, has become, in a sense, consubstantial with public and political life. Most protagonists in political life project their own representation of Sharia as well as the use they intend to make of it in public life, where this representation is supposed to be seen as the expression of the self-evident. Opinions about the content of Sharia vary considerably, but it has become difficult, in the contemporary Muslim world, to position oneself outside the space defined by Sharia. It is admittedly only a framework, but the framework of a sieve through which every discourse seems to be filtered.

10

Sharia in Countries Where Islam is in a Minority

Globalization and migrations have had a major impact on the manner in which different religions and ways of living one's faith are mixed together. Dogmas and practices of populations of diverse origins have been so profoundly affected that numerous local traditions have been 'globalized'. The local religiosities of Muslim migrants have been shuffled and mixed, and countries of residence have become crucibles for the emergence of new forms of expression of faith, of relation to the Islamic norm and to tradition. Often what is lumped together as 'popular religiosity' has seen its particular features fade in favour of more homogeneous and non-native ways of formulating rules of dress, diet, sexuality, and morality. In this respect, certain currents of thought have been able to impose their vision of Islam and its norms, to the extent of making them the new versions of orthodoxy. Sharia did not escape this dynamic – to which, up to a certain point, it owes its return to popularity. This phenomenon has distilled a standardized and doubtless impoverished decoction, which seems at the same time to possess the virtue of being multi-functional in the areas of law, politics, ethics, discourse, media, and identity.

The presence of Muslims in countries where the majority of the population does not practise Islam has led to the emergence of numerous questions. Some are legal in character and concern the recognition of national laws inspired by Islamic norms in largely secular states. Others are linked to the practice by believers of their religion and the possibility of living and practising their faith in societies where reference to human rights and the principle of the religious neutrality of the state predominate. In this case the question of Islamic normativity often acquires a moral dimension. It is a question of knowing how to live in conformity with one's convictions in situations where they are not necessarily shared by the majority of the population. Outside Muslim-majority societies one can also use Sharia as a marker of identity, and it can also have a political significance. The supposed content of its rules is therefore assumed to define the contours of a community based on religious affiliation and on the rejection of the secular order. Sharia is also an object of discussion in the media, in Western society, within secularized systems of law, by people who do not claim adherence to it for themselves, but make suppositions about its nature and ascribe observance of it to others.

Openings in private international law

Under the impact of migration, above all else, the legal systems of Western countries have been confronted with otherness and difference. This encounter with legal rules and diverse codes of normativity coincides with the emergence of nation-states and the development of their own legal systems. The construction of a codified national legal system was an undertaking of rationalization as much as of centralization. For this reason the experience was a success at a global level inasmuch as it offered a new technique of arranging social relations.

The proliferation of national laws has led to the establishment of dispensations that allow the resolution of conflict between laws. There are, in fact, situations where multiple national laws, which may contradict one another, are susceptible of being applied. Private international law is a branch of the internal law of each state which settles the conflicts that can arise from the existence of elements linked to a foreign legal system. Through techniques that enable these contradictions to be resolved, certain elements of the law of one state can be taken into consideration and applied in another. Thus, for example, provisions of Moroccan family law can be taken into consideration by a Belgian magistrate who has to resolve a conflict about the maintenance allowance for the children of a couple resident in Belgium, but married under Moroccan law and in the process of divorce. From this point of view, and to the extent that Moroccan law refers, in matters of personal status, to Islam and the Maliki school, one observes that there is a possibility, albeit indirect, for Sharia to have a legal existence in a context to which it seems at first sight foreign. But, and this should be emphasized, it is never in the name of Islam that private international law is applied, but solely through the national law of a country whose legal system can have an Islamic inspiration. In practical terms this means that only Muslims of a nationality other than that of the state where the dispute is examined are able to benefit from application of the laws of their country of origin.

The family law of Muslim-majority countries can be applied in Western countries when foreigners coming from the former, who have settled through immigration, marry, divorce, inherit, or have a child, for example. Numerous European countries agree, by virtue of the rules of conflict of laws and jurisdictions, that the national law of foreigners can be applied, particularly in family matters. Occasionally, that provokes tensions arising from opposition between values. In this kind of situation, the notion of public order is invoked to reject the foreign law. Recourse to this notion is principally by magistrates. The exception of public order allows the rejection of foreign rules, those of Islamic inspiration among others, such as a wife's duty of obedience, repudiation, polygamy, the forbidding of marriage between a Muslim woman and a non-Muslim man, the unilateral revocation of repudiation by a husband during the waiting period after divorce, or the absence of consent to marriage by a prospective wife.[1] However, recourse to this notion is attenuated if a judge considers that it is preferable to protect the interest of persons seen as vulnerable, particularly wives and children. It is thus that judges can sometimes recognize certain aspects of polygamous unions, such as the establishment of filiation with regard to children, the right to upkeep, the right to maintenance obligations among spouses, the right to share a retirement pension or a succession right, and the possibility for two widows to both obtain damages following the accidental death of their common husband.

In reality, although many European judges recognize the relevance, in principle, of foreign legal systems, in virtue of the rules governing conflict between laws, they do not apply it. Often, it is because of a lack of knowledge of foreign law and the expenses involved in in-depth research into the applicable systems. This is also the expression of a general tendency towards decline in the application of the criterion of nationality in favour of that of the usual place of residence of those concerned. With regard to divorce or maintenance obligations, for example, when the two spouses are domiciled in France, it is French law that is applied (with the notable exception of Moroccan law, which is applied in virtue of the Convention of 1981).

The perception by magistrates of the situation prevailing in Belgium can help to illustrate this question. They first insist that there is a close link between migration and the application of foreign national laws inspired by Islamic norms. They do not in general contest the legitimacy of this application and thus that of private international law, but lament the difficulty, in terms of time, access, and competence, in knowing exactly which rules from these foreign laws should be put into practice. The temptation can then arise to automatically apply Belgian law or to systematically invoke the public order exception, which renders the foreign law inoperable.[2]

Personal status and Islamic norm in a secularized public space

People originally from Muslim-majority countries are often no longer migrants, in the strict sense of the term. They have definitively settled, they can have dual nationality, and their life and sense of belonging are essentially local. This development modifies the legal situation fairly radically, in the sense that the provisions of foreign national laws no longer apply, but only those of the countries – France, Sweden, the United States, etc. – whose nationality these communities hold. The questions that are raised concern, consequently, the domain of cultural, moral, and religious norms which these people wish to respect. As a whole, these rules do not pose any particular legal problem – the practice of fasting during the month of Ramadan does not clash with any provision of Belgian law, for example, and there is therefore no reason for any magistrate to be concerned with it. Any debate that does arise has its origins in political and social manoeuvres at a national level, with the mixture of manipulation and provocation that that entails: one can think of the 'wine and pork' aperitifs organized by right and left secular extremism. There are differences between legal rules and religious norms in other fields, but they seem manageable. To take only one example, it should therefore be possible to find an accommodation between the different conceptions of the act of marriage.

There remains, finally, a series of situations in which it is more problematic to reconcile legal rules and religious convictions. It would, however, be reductionist to adopt a merely legalistic reflex that excludes all forms of accommodation between a secular order and Islamic norms. If only for reasons of civil peace and social cohesion, every effort should be made to avoid a polarization which could lead to the development of strategies to skirt around national law, whether by organizing a parallel community life, as in the case of religious marriages contracted without taking account of any recognition by national law, or by having recourse to the law of a foreign country which is more accommodating on these questions, such as the marriages formalized in Morocco by Belgian citizens originally from Morocco, several generations ago. 'These two forms of marginalization present serious disadvantages; informal marriage will not be recognized by the civil authorities and thus leaves one or other of the spouses vulnerable; solutions obtained abroad, for their part, create a legal privilege benefiting the citizens of Muslim countries … while the links with the country where civil law prevails … have strengthened over the years, too strong to be able to claim a recourse to private international law.'[3]

There are lines of inquiry to explore in order to avoid this polarization while respecting the secular legal framework. One way is to allow the integration into civil law of provisions inspired by Islam, using the field of contractual procedure. The spouses could, for example, conclude a valid civil contract containing clauses that would enable them to arrange their union, respecting the norms of their religion and without infringing the fundamental rights of either spouse. A second approach would be, with the aim of accommodating religious convictions, to extend the existing option to use the law of their country of origin rather than that of their country of residence, but always on the condition that the solution does not compromise the fundamental rights of either party.

The third approach involves arbitration techniques in certain family-related matters. It is a procedural solution, which enables a certain number of disputes to be submitted to arbitration forums composed of people with religious competence and legitimacy. The British experience merits mention. In the context of the Arbitration Act of 1996, arbitration forums are authorized to offer their services to Muslims who wish to use them in family disputes. The objective is to find an alternative way of resolving conflicts while maintaining the requirements of individual rights, fundamental rights, and procedural guarantees. In other words, a space is opened for an Islamic mode of arbitration, but within a controlled framework. We can note that this practice does not reproduce traditional institutions, but is a new way of settling disputes between Muslims which respects the pre-eminence of resorting to religion and the authority of scholars versed in the canonical texts.

However, there is no single Western system any more than there is one Islamic disposition, and each national context is extremely specific. British society is fairly receptive to the principle of community organization, as well as to the role of religion and the family, but things are very different in the countries of continental Europe, where social homogeneity is more of an established value and state law is disinclined to accept the authority of autonomous institutions. The experience of the British Shariah Councils is evidence of this. These are not arbitration structures set up in the framework of the Arbitration Act, but are religious institutions created locally, parallel to (but not necessarily against) the law in response to a community need to regulate questions and disputes without recourse to the legal structures of the state. The best known is the Islamic Shariah Council of London, which currently deals with around 600 divorce cases each year. Doubtless this raises difficult issues, particularly with regard to the equality and protection of women. However, one has to recognize that such institutions enjoy noteworthy success, even among women, who often find that certain of their needs are met through these institutions in a more efficient and rapid manner.[4] What is manifestly clear is the need to ground its conceptualization in the terrain of people's practical concerns rather than leaving it at the ethereal and unresolvable level of principles.

When Islam becomes Western

There is another way by which elements of Islamic normativity can establish themselves or provoke debate in a context where non-Muslims are in the majority. The fundamental rights recognizing liberty of conscience and the freedom of worship create, in fact, the possibility for Islamic provisions that are more religious and ethical than legal to be recognized and protected. This is the case for matters as diverse as the places of prayer, foodstuffs produced in a manner that conforms to ritual, or dress. These questions can generate polemics which crystallize various debates quickly labeled as identity driven, in which the definition and extension of the pluralism of contemporary democratic societies are at stake. Whether in Europe or in North America, the social and legal acceptance of practices and behaviour historically foreign, *a fortiori* when associated with a minority, constitutes a major issue, all the more so given that these societies have constructed and present themselves to the world on a principle of universality. It is thus in the name of the ideology of human rights – and their universal and secular character – and of the positive law of the modern nation-state that an opening is made in the direction of Islamic norms. It is no longer a matter of classical Islamic doctrine or law associated with Islam. It is a third type of scenario, where a legal system is unconcerned by Islam but needs, by its own internal logic, to recognize certain indirect effects of Islamic normativity.

A reference to Islam has therefore developed within the European context, as distinct from transnational movements. Tensions have been revealed between pretentions to state neutrality, secularized religious values, traditionally dominant religions, and postmodernity. Western societies and states have been confronted with the underpinnings of their own cultures and the expectations implicit in their structures – in legal terms among others – as well as the relativity of their 'universal' aspirations and the demons of identity which never emerge so clearly as in times of crisis. 'Highlighting this genealogy of Western law, the Islamic reference reopens a tension whose resolution is unclear between an internal public order redefined in a pluralistic fashion and thus open to a process of reception, and a public order which will foreground its identity-focused basis and thus close in on itself.'[5]

It is important to stress that, for a secular state and its legal system, recognizing a religion such as Islam in no way entails application of that religion's norms. Belgian law, for example, recognizes the Islamic faith, but that does not mean that institutions such as polygamy and repudiation are *ipso facto* accepted – far from it. Islam is recognized as a religion with representative authorities in precisely defined roles, but they have no legislative power capable of introducing new rules into the Belgian legal system.

Islam is above all a religious entity, and thus eventually a religious norm, and not a legal entity. This is something that it is not always easy to understand, because of confusion created by the invention of the notion of 'Islamic law', which affects both Muslims and non-Muslims, and includes judges involved in a dispute where Islam is at stake. In some circumstances a judge may take the responsibility of defining the legal aspect of a religious prescription, even though the prescription has no legal standing and the judge has no religious authority. This phenomenon is reinforced by the tendency to simplify, homogenize, and stereotype Islam as well as those who identify with it or to whom a Muslim identity is attributed. People are surprised if a Muslim, or someone who is supposed to be Muslim, drinks a glass of wine, because of the legal and religious framework to which this person is assigned. Something that is a matter of social relationships can become a legal issue if the stereotype is crystallized in the ruling of a judge. It is also frequent to speak of Islam and the Muslim community in the singular, with all the significant consequences this can have for the representations of Muslims and the impressions non-Muslims can thus have of this religion and identity.

Individual autonomy, which is a justification for declaring one's adherence to a religion, its precepts, and constraining norms, must sometimes be subjected to a test of sincerity and credibility when it is invoked as the basis of a conscientious exception with regard to the legal obligations of a secular state. One cannot accept the caprices of individual opinion any more than one can agree automatically to all the demands of a communitarian movement. Such a task is undertaken as much by the state authorities, which have to strive for the establishment of a functional pluralism, as by individuals and groups who affirm their commitment to Islam and its prescriptions. The requirements of their religion must have as their aim the following of religious faith, and not political confrontation. The European Court of Human Rights has judged that, with regard to questions of this sort, not every type of conduct determined by religion is automatically subject to protection. Only the central and essential part of a conviction can be guaranteed, on condition that it is not contrary to public order, that it can be reasonably anticipated, and can be in harmony with coexistence in a democratic society.

If a judge is led to give credit to a religious claim, that does not mean that religious law takes precedence over national laws, but only that religion can motivate people's acts, and thus can sometimes be recognized as an excuse and justification for behaviour which would otherwise be viewed as breaking a law, or constituting an exception to it.

It is thus that a judge can allow that the wearing of a headscarf is the object of a sufficiently strong religious conviction to justify an exception to a ban on religious symbols in the school environment. Such a decision, without making the headscarf a legal obligation in any way, enables a religious element to be given a certain place within a pluralist system.

Europe is not the only place where Islam is practised in a minority setting. In India and China, very sizeable Muslim populations must find ways of living within a state for which Islam constitutes at best one recognized religion among others. In North America the Muslim community is also significant in number, and there as elsewhere Islam has come to occupy a prominent place in public debate. Leaving aside the polemics targeting Islam, one has to acknowledge that Islam's treatment in the legal sphere is often less problematic and less subject to special treatment than is the case in Europe. Conflicts relating to family law are treated by tribunals on a case-by-case basis, with markedly less surrounding emotion than is the case in Europe. American judges have a tendency to take a pragmatic approach, seeking elements in the precepts of Islamic family doctrine that can be interpreted in liberal, secularized terms. Thus in North America, 'the distinction which appears the most clearly is not the so-called conflict between Islamic law and secular law, or the competition between two "models" of resolution of conflict. The most striking difference is rather that which separates the attitude of legal professionals (lawyers, judges, theorists of the constitution) and that of public opinion and organizations which defend the rights of minorities.[6]

Islamic doctrine in minority situations

As Sharia is not a legal system but a system of norms it is not surprising that it goes beyond the legal domain which, since the nineteenth century, has had a tendency to simultaneously limit and absorb it. It is among other things a means of framing piety and its rituals, as well as a repertoire of political engagement and social, cultural, and identity affirmation. In minority settings this has given rise to questions on the ways of life of *Homo islamicus* outside the Muslim context. It is possible to present a brief typology of the discursive reality constituted by Sharia in the European context.[7]

The first position adopted is one of literalism. From this perspective, the religious Norm constituted by Sharia offers an adequate and instant solution to the troubles of the age. 'Muslims are convinced of the necessity at every time and in every place, of returning to divine law. In its rigour they see the sign of divine pity. This conviction is not sustained by blind fanaticism but by realism which correspond to the nature of life.'[8] Inversely, the Sharia can become a focus of reformist effort which includes taking a critical distance from it. It can even lead to rejecting it purely and simply, as the only means of 'reconciling Muslims today with their religion'.[9] From this perspective, referring to Sharia is presented as anachronistic, a danger to freedom, and regressive to the extent that it prevents the pursuit of the hermeneutic work that is indispensable to the development of a modern Islam.

Between these extreme positions there are various suggestions which call for the adaptation of Sharia to the specific conditions of Muslim life in Europe. Thus Tareq Oubrou, the imam of the Grand Mosque in Bordeaux, has elaborated a 'modified theory of the Sharia which aims at reconciling religious law and European forms of secularism'.[10] This 'minimalist orthodoxy' limits the Sharia to questions of religious practice and moral principles, and seeks to remove any legal dimension from it. The aim is to construct a 'minority Sharia': 'The term minority puts Sharia in context, and thus responds to the French secular situation among others. This means relating the norm to the prevailing situation while remaining faithful to the methods that govern the application of Sharia to reality. Reality determines the specific form assumed by particular regulation from Sharia, or even its non-applicability in certain cases.'[11] The 'doctrine of minorities' is an expanding field of discourse about the situation of Muslim communities in minority contexts. Nearly a third of the world's Muslim population, in fact, lives in countries where they form a religious minority. While life in a non-Muslim context may present no particular problems for many people who are 'sociologically' Muslims, it is very different for those who see themselves as being required to live according to their religious Norm. Such people believe that the principles that prevailed in former times for communities abandoned to unbelieving rulers after the retreat of Muslim armies should be extended to modern Muslim communities. The doctrine relating to minorities is not limited to this fairly radical type; it has numerous contrasting facets, and offers pragmatic, casuistic solutions which differ from each other with regard to questions relating to food, clothing, marriage, and coexistence with non-Muslims.

The Sharia can also be given a symbolic dimension in discourse about its place and vocation in the Western context. Here the aim is to go beyond the usual debates by re-reading it in a secular context or searching for its spiritual essence. For the Islamic thinker Tariq Ramadan Islam in Europe is simultaneously a 'link to the transcendent' and a 'vector of social justice' through the Sharia.[12] The legal value is therefore removed from Sharia and it becomes the 'path of fidelity to the objectives of Islam'. Ramadan adds: 'All laws which protect life and human dignity promote justice and equality, and impose respect for nature, and similar values, all these laws are *my Sharia* applied in *my* society, even if it is not Muslim in majority or if these laws have not been thought of or produced by Muslim scholars.'[13]

Virtuous abstraction, disciplinary order, political slogans

Rather than struggling to define the essence of things, it seems important to seek what they mean when they are invoked. That does not tell us what the thing is, but what people associate with the thing. This agnostic posture enables us to understand human phenomena instead of imposing a transcendental and intangible truth. With regard to Sharia, everyone seems constantly obsessed by its definition. It is true of those who make a target of Sharia as well as of the guardians of the Law who claim to know the Norm in its timeless truth. However, if one looks closer, Sharia is often nothing more than a 'virtuous abstraction', that is to say, a slogan with positive moral connotations: what Muslims need; everything that is good for them; the Islamic conception of the Good.[14] It matters little, in a certain sense, what that means in practical terms, but Sharia is no longer understood here as a collection of specific and precisely constraining rules, but as an identity-related reference embodying the virtue of the 'Islamic way'.

Those who want to identify with this virtuous abstraction will often privilege certain sectors of ordinary life, on which they concentrate their ethical militancy. These domains are those of ritual, finance, family relations, and social relations. They have only a tenuous connection with the positive law of Western states. The question of sexual relations outside marriage, for example, receives massive attention from the supporters of the application of Sharia, while legal opinion has broadly disengaged from the question. Islamic finance is perceived as the means of respecting the Quranic prohibition of usury, but its implementation consists of an offer of banking products whose legality does not have its origins in religious considerations. The respect for certain dietary interdictions or rules relating to the slaughter of animals is a matter only for believers, not legislators, as long as public regulations in the domain of hygiene are respected. The law is completely indifferent to relations between religious confessions, apart from condemning discriminatory practices that go against the principle of equality.

These areas of Sharia belong to morality rather than to law. It is a system, or even a disciplinary obsession. It involves regulating one's life as a believer according to the precepts of a revealed Norm. It does not concern those who could be described as 'sociological Muslims', for whom Islam is more about an ancestry, a familiarity, and a community. Sharia thus understood concerns practising Muslims who aspire to 'orthopraxis' – that is to say, conformity between their daily practices and religious norms. We are in a domain where the individual will of believers guarantees the execution of actions which they see as obligatory, recommended, blameworthy, or forbidden.

The call for Sharia has also often become an identity-related demand, a rallying point for those who live in a sort of pluralism where majority and minority cultures coexist and who construct the 'object' Sharia as a point of convergence for everything that might seem to constitute their 'being-in-society': marriage, circumcision, burial, festivals, Ramadan, diet, and so on. We are not dealing with orthopraxis here, because people's relationship with religious rules is more flexible, occasional, and cultural. Sharia constitutes a general norm which provides a framework for the organization of such events in a more or less vague fashion, regardless of whether they derive from Islamic prescriptions or local custom. One encounters again the idea of virtuous abstraction, except that this conception of Sharia does not involve only practising and convinced believers but also 'sociological Muslims' who may not believe but who nevertheless wish to observe a certain number of precepts traditionally associated with Islam.

The Islamist phenomenon has in large part been developed as a reaction to culture and lifestyle in Western countries, with the aim of making them either the antithesis of the ideal Islamic city or the embodiment of the impiety that has to be fought. That does not mean, for all that, that certain aspects of modernity are not appropriated, openly or otherwise, by movements that have contrasting appreciations of the balance that should be achieved between the objective constituted by the ideal Islamic society and the means employed to attain it. Moreover, Islamism, in all its elements, has taken root in Western countries, both through communities from different countries and as a means of transcending national divisions. The organizations representing Muslim communities, in France or elsewhere, often reflect the dominant political or national influences. As soon as Islamism is involved, the reference to Sharia becomes omnipresent, as we saw in the preceding chapter. However, both in countries where Muslims are a majority and where they are a minority, Sharia is a discursive tool rather than a corpus of universally defined regulations. In a radical version, the Sharia4 movement, in all its various manifestations (Europe, Belgium, the UK), does not propose more than what is enunciated in the organization's title: a call for the application of Sharia in Europe, in the United Kingdom, in Belgium, and so on.

It is tempting, in conclusion, to place in the same category the various caricatural conceptions of Sharia sustained by the extremes of the Western political spectrum. These extremes share a literalist and reductionist vision of Sharia, conceived as a collection of restrictive prescriptions in family matters (polygamy, repudiation, the authority of husbands), penal ordinances (corporal punishments), and political projects (the revival of the caliphate). This vision is morally polarized, between the Sharia as representing virtue and as an object of criticism. The Lille marriage affair, in which a judge was asked to annul a marriage after the bridegroom discovered that his bride was not a virgin, constitutes a good example of the double nature of this polarized conception of Sharia. On the one hand, a man, following his own conception of Sharia, insists that the virginity of the woman he marries is a substantive condition of the marriage. On the other, public opinion, whipped up by the media, imputes to Sharia a discriminatory imperative which is unacceptable in French society. The question is not problematic in law: it is perfectly permissible for persons contracting a marriage to insist on substantive conditions which, if not respected, render the marriage invalid. This was, indeed, the opinion of the judge of the court of first instance. In politics, on the other hand, it is more complicated. Once the spectre of the application of Sharia in France has been evoked, it becomes difficult not to act, even when it is legally unjustifiable. This is why the minister of justice instructed the prosecutor to lodge an appeal.[15]

In all of this, the Sharia is not prominent as a collection of substantive rules, and is even sometimes completely absent. However, Sharia as a positive or negative moral reference is central. Having been constructed as Islamic law, then removed more or less completely from the law of Islamic countries, it is now inscribed durably in the moral horizon of populations linked in one way or another to Islam. More than ever, it seems that what Sharia is matters little: what counts is what one makes of it. Almost all these configurations are imaginable. All tell us more about those who design them and those to whom they are attributed than they do about Sharia itself. Like reflections in a mirror the Sharia slips away, escapes, returns, but never lets itself be caught.

Conclusion

The source of the confusion surrounding the answers given to a particular problematic is often to be found in the way that problematic is envisaged. Such is assuredly the case of everything to do with Islam and Muslims, starting with the very idea of 'Muslim societies'. Why does this label have to be given to societies whose identities are plural and vary according to their particular regional and national histories? Is it a convenient linguistic term to characterize a certain number of peoples who are 'different' from 'us'? But in this case one must emphasize that as a description 'Muslim' has no explicative value. In addition, the use of a convenient linguistic term to define the other ought rather to lead us to wonder what point of view is adopted to consider the 'other' rather than the reality of the 'other' constructed by this point of view. If the other is the object of our questioning, we have to 'decentre' our perception and try to accede to the categories of belonging as they function for those who employ them, and refuse to take our world as the measure of everything.

Without such a critique of our way of thinking we thicken the fog instead of dissipating it. This is what happens when one claims that the religious and the political are mixed together in Islam or that Sharia is the touchstone of the coming of modernity in Muslim societies. The equation that makes Islam an amalgam of 'religion and world and state' (*din dunya dawla*) is a doctrinal construction and not a genetic property of Islam, only of the reified and essentialized Islam which unites the two sides of the same coin constituted by Islamic orthodoxy and Orientalist science. In reality, an attentive reading of history reveals far more frequently that temporal power and spiritual magisterium are uncoupled one from another rather than blended together. Both essentialist perspectives ('Islam *is* this or that') and sociological perspectives ('Islam can be reduced to what Muslims do') lead nowhere: the question of the relations between 'Islam' and 'politics' or 'Sharia' and 'democracy' is meaningless in such general terms, and any answer to a question made up of chimeras is quite simply absurd.

All through this book we have insisted that the question 'What is the Sharia?' should provoke another question – that is, 'What is Sharia *made to be*?' This response cannot of course be met with approval by any dogmatic style of thinking, irritating literalists and frustrating positivists of every kind. It is not the basis for any kind of apologetic nor does it fuel the discourse of the critics of Islam. Islam is neither a being nor an essence, and its law does not escape this truth. Islam is a human reality, and can only be spoken of in these terms, outside faith-based discourse at least. The relationship to the Sharia is not the dominant imponderable about 'Muslim societies'. On the one hand, Sharia does not determine all the behaviour of the people composing these societies; on the other, there is no direct connection between the social life of the twenty-first century and the historical Prophetic period, while it is not possible for 'Islamic peoples' to be in tune with the contemporary world. Sharia is not schizophrenic, caught between tradition and modernity, between a conservative past and a progressive present. Asking about the compatibility between Islam and modernity can lead to a type of answer which is simultaneously positive and negative, since both possibilities can be defended. Let it be clear that these opposing versions are the two sides of the same coin which claims that Islam represents something in itself, independently of what humans make of it.

A religion and its norm are not only tradition or memory, supposing that they are a single homogeneous thing and not concepts enabling us to use a single term to designate phenomena which belong to the same family. Islam and Sharia are at the same time a corpus of founding texts and ways of referring to these texts. They are also a constellation of practices of all kinds, where faith, wisdom, morality, ideology, routine, politics, ethics, truth, justice, and many other things coexist and compete with each other. Before it is a tradition, Islam is an act of faith, a faith which finds in the Sharia a normative framework leading to Salvation. This faith has an extraordinarily complex elaboration, but it is quite simply false to think, on the pretext that the disenchantment of the world is more or less complete, that belief is not primordial or that it is only a superstructure barely concealing conflictual relations between generations, social classes, sexes, or races. Religion as ideology is supplementary to pre-existing faith, serving as political confirmation of preceding moral and religious conviction. From this point of view, in addition, one should treat with caution psychological-style explanations which see in religion a kind of bricolage enabling people to console themselves in the face of life's vicissitudes. There is certainly a religious sentiment which proceeds from an individual and collective experience and does not play a merely functional role.

A religion is a 'heterogeneous reality, contradictory, polymorphous, and rich in nuance'.[1] It is not one thing but several, and does not fulfil one function but different functions (and sometimes none), functions which can be contradictory and yet exercised simultaneously. In this sense a religion is not the root of a society or a civilization, but one of its multiple components. As previously mentioned, it is a convenient linguistic term, sometimes a family name, and in this case too, it is the object of many language games. If it is not an essence or a matrix, a religion does not have a particular destiny, and its history has a finality only when one looks backwards from the present into the past. Religion proceeds in a sequence of steps, an epigenesis, and 'is constituted through time in a gradual unforeseeable way'.[2] It is an intellectual illusion to believe that ideas make history and not the contrary. It is to give too much credit to political thought to claim that it fashions the destiny of the state. At best, political thought accompanies the development of the state, giving people living at a particular time the means to frame and accept what is imposed by actual events.

Today one can be an Islamist, talk about Sharia, and accept pluralism, human rights, and the sanctions of the ballot box. The question of the Islamists' double language is a cliché, and their profession of faith in democracy should suffice until the contrary can be proved. This trial of intent is, in addition, as insoluble as it is vain: how can the duplicity of the Islamists be proved – as well as, by the way, the sincerity of their detractors? If the Arab Spring has shown anything, it is not the incompatibility of Islam and democracy or Sharia and human rights, but rather the difficulty of improvising new ways of practising politics when one has neither the experience nor the competence. The blockages one can observe in certain societies and regions of the world do not come from a sclerotic doctrine. The contrary is the case: the problematic circumstances of these societies produce a doctrine incapable of renewal.

With regard to Islam and the Sharia there is a strong tendency to produce a narrative which is retrospective, normative, and all-embracing, putting *a posteriori* in coherent form events whose unity is, *a priori*, very relative.

Producing such a master narrative, one establishes relations between disjointed occurrences, a chain of causality between independent facts; a historical meaning is given to contingent events and judgements are made about coherence, success, and reality (or their opposites: incoherence, failure, and illusion), about entities to which people assign a finality, a project, or an intention. One of the consequences of this attitude is, in the guise of analysis, to produce what is in fact a formalized justification of a judgement that has been previously established. It is the classic image of the windmill that Don Quixote imagines as an enemy in order to charge at it. A finality is established so that things can be evaluated in terms of their contribution to its realization. A project is selected so that evaluations can be made in the light of its accomplishment. An intention is articulated so that one can judge whether or not the objective has been established. The study of Islam and of Muslim societies is heavily affected by this Don Quixote-style syndrome. Mirroring the theses of the inexorable victory of Islamism, discourse has proliferated on its failure and decline. Islamism has been presented as a vector of rupture with modernity, or, inversely, as a vector of entry into modernity. This cyclical conception of the movements of Islamic history found new vigour with the Arab Spring, where the triumphal march of secularization, youth, Islamic democracy, or cyber-society was prophesied. All of this is based on highly problematic conceptions of religion and history.

First, the conception of religion is problematic. One can in reality ask oneself if these 'returns to religion' are really rather an 'adaptation of belief to the modern conditions of social and personal life'.[3] In this sense there is neither an apogee nor a decline of Islamism, but the constant reformulation of the relations of people, whether Muslim or not, to belief and to their surroundings. Thinking about Islam only in terms of Islamism limits one's view of the many processes operating at levels other than the political, such as that at which people privilege acts of devotion, literalist applications of rules, and patterns of behaviour which conform to an idea of the Golden Age. More observation is needed of how these processes act in concert with Islamism and may therefore ultimately have an effect on the way that power is understood and exercised. It is not enough to object that Islamism is an ideology whereas Islam is a religion. The frontiers between ideology, morality, metaphysics, and politics are very difficult to establish, and politics can be influenced by the reconfigurations of public morality. It is therefore false to believe that political actors veer between self-delusion ('they manipulate Islam for political ends') and constant Machiavellianism ('he is only an opportunistic Muslim'). One is a Muslim first, and it is only secondarily that one thinks of Islam in political terms.

These misunderstandings are also due to a problematic conception of history. Sometimes the world is given a direction, an evolution, a finality – in short, a teleology –

that of secularization and disenchantment, which Islamism sought, it is claimed, to overthrow, before finally conforming and transforming itself into Islamic democracy. On other occasions it is claimed that the world is confronted with the cyclical movement of history, governed by eternal recommencement. By attributing a revolutionary project to political movements, for example, one can evaluate what they have not achieved among the objectives they assigned themselves and thus conclude that they have failed or that they were illusory in nature. In so doing, however, one loses sight of the fact that the revolutionary project was not so much an actual project for these movements as a project that was attributed to them. If political movements aspire to anything it is, in general, to oppose the ruling regime and to replace it. It is in any case a constant feature of Islamism, across the spectrum of its manifestations, as numerous as they are distinct from one another. Beyond hollow and repetitive slogans such as 'Islam is the solution' it is very difficult to ascribe to them a precise political project, apart from that of acceding to power. In these conditions it is a strange process which claims that these movements have failed to realize an ideological process that they have never had. The only failure that lies in wait for them is that of not acceding to power, or, having acceded to power, to then lose it.

If, in France and Europe, people take an interest in Sharia, it is because there is a prevailing obsession with

Islam and Muslims, for reasons that seem objective but which often depend on the way that we frame questions. In this sense, the mode of construction of that discourse is central. As Islam and Sharia are fixed in and through public debate, the capacity to impose one's point of view as the authoritative one has become crucial. Directly at stake is power, its conquest, and its conservation, since electoral 'market shares' are involved.

Such discourse is often, by a sort of mirror effect, the counter-narrative of another narrative. The *'ulama* recount that the Sharia is an ideal leading those who follow it to Salvation. The narrative of the opponents of Islam is that Sharia is an evil which makes its adherents the source of numerous ills afflicting the world. In both cases the Sharia is a thing-in-itself which necessarily determines the nature and actions of those who follow it. The moral of the tale is evidently very different according to the version one chooses and the distribution of roles, between the forces of good and the forces of evil that each version involves. And as these two moral attributes are mutually exclusive, the heroes of one story are the villains of the other. The production of this kind of discourse, which makes a claim for exclusive truth, constitutes a powerful political tool in the hands of activists with marked populist propensities. They aim to make a version of the truth seem natural, in such a way that it presents itself as if it were self-evident, constructing an authoritative vision of things and drawing political consequences from this. This is the way of the world! It is, however, clearly not the task of analysts, based on the authority of their knowledge, to support any of these versions or intensify these consequences.

Notes

Introduction

1. A glossary of specific terms used in this work in French or Arabic is found on pp. 229–34.
2. Bruno Étienne, *L'islamisme radical*, Paris: Hachette, 1988, p. 7.
3. Georges Corm, *L'Europe et l'Orient: de la Balkanisation à la libéralisation*. Histoire d'une modernité inaccomplie, Paris: La Découverte, 1989, p. 372.
4. Maxime Rodinson, *La Fascination de l'islam*, Paris: La Découverte, 1990, p. 193.

1
A Concept and Its Contexts

1. Baudouin Dupret, *Au nom de quel droit: répertoires juridiques et référence religieuse dans la société égyptienne musulmane contemporaine*, Paris: LDGJ, 2000, p. 10.
2. Quoted by Robert Gleave, 'La charia dans l'histoire: ijtihad, épistémologie et "Tradition classique"', in Baudouin Dupret (ed.), *La charia aujourd'hui: usages de la référence au droit islamique*, Paris: La Découverte, 2012, p. 24.
3. Oussama Arabi, *Studies in Modern Islamic Law and Jurisprudence*, The Hague/London/New York: Kluwer Law International, 2001.
4. Mohammed Hocine Benkheira, *Islam et interdits alimentaires, juguler l'animalité*, Paris: PUF, 2000.
5. Ibid., p. 8.
6. Wael Hallaq, *Shari'a: Theory, Practice, Transformations*, Cambridge: Cambridge University Press, 2009.
7. Ibid., p. 361.

219

8.   Ibid., p. 362.
9.   Ibid., p. 364.
10. Ibid., p. 363.
11. Ibid., p. 365.
12. Bernard Lewis, *Le langage politique de l'islam*, Paris: Gallimard, 1988.
13. Ali Mezghani, *L'État inachevé: la question du droit dans les pays arabes*, Paris: Gallimard, 2011, p. 297.
14. Gleave, 'La charia dans l'histoire', pp. 25–6.
15. Jean-Noël Ferrié, 'Usages politiques de la charia', in Dupret (ed.), *La charia aujourd'hui*, p. 89.

2
Exploring the Sources of the Divine Law: The Quran

1.   The origin of the name of the reigning dynasty in Jordan, the Hashemites.
2.   The name of the most famous Arab Muslim tribe.
3.   This is the basis for the prohibition of adoption in the contemporary legal systems of Muslim-majority countries.
4.   Orientalist literature is that which seeks to study the civilizations of the East from the viewpoint of an outside (Western) observer.
5.   Christian Décobert, *Le mendiant et le combattant: l'institution de l'islam*, Paris: Le Seuil, 1991, p. 26.
6.   'Abdelilah al-'Ajami, *Que dit vraiment le Coran*, Aubagne: Éditions Zenith, 2011.
7.   'Abd al-Qadir 'Awda, *al-Islam wa awda'una al-qanuniyya*, Cairo: n.p., n.d.
8.   Joseph Schacht, *An Introduction to Islamic Law*, Oxford: Oxford University Press, 1964, p. 11.
9.   Décobert, *Le mendiant et le combattant*, p. 27.
10. Hervé Bleuchot, *Droit musulman*, vol. I: *Histoire*, Aix-en-Provence: PUAM, 2000, pp. 54–7.
11. The waiting period corresponds to that during which a woman who is widowed or divorced cannot remarry, often to avoid doubt over paternity in case of pregnancy.
12. Mohammad Ali Amir-Moezzi, *Le Coran silencieux et le Coran parlant: sources scripturaires de l'islam entre histoire et ferveur*, Paris: CNRS, 2011.

13. The Kharijites were a dissident sect of Islam which emerged out of the conflict between the caliph 'Ali and the Umayyad Mu'awiya in the aftermath of the arbitration after the Battle of Siffin in 657.
14. Décobert, *Le mendiant et le combattant*, p. 27.
15. Ibn Khaldun, *Muqaddima*, VI, 10.
16. Maxime Rodinson, *Mahomet*, Paris: Le Seuil, 1961, pp. 119–20.
17. The Egyptian civil law code stipulates that a Muslim Egyptian woman can only marry a man of the Muslim confession, and obliges her to divorce him if he loses this status because of apostasy.

3
The Sources of the Divine Norm: Prophetic Tradition

1   Décobert, *Le mendiant et le combattant*, p. 47.
2.   Ibid., p. 306.
3.   Schacht, *Introduction to Islamic Law*, p. 32.
4.   Dupret, *Au nom de quel droit*, p. 208.
5.   Ministerial Decree No. 261 of 1996.

4
Access to Sharia: Consensus and Analogical Reasoning

1.   For example, the maxim that 'the child belongs to the marriage bed', signifying that descent is defined by birth within wedlock.
2.   Translation into French by Charles Pellat, quoted in Bleuchot, *Droit musulman*, vol. I, p. 84.
3.   Noel Coulson, *A History of Islamic Law*, London: Translation Paperbacks, 2011, p. 31.
4.   Hallaq, *Sharīʿa: Theory, Practice, Transformations*, p. 101.
5.   Quran III, 104: 'And let there be [arising] from you a nation inviting to [all that is] good, enjoining what is right and forbidding what is wrong, and those will be the successful.'
6.   Hallaq, *Sharia: Theory, Practice, Transformations*, p. 106.
7.   Coulson, *A History of Islamic Law*, p. 39.
8.   The inverted commas indicate that this appellation dates from a later period. Up until the time of the early Umayyads the term used was 'the Commander of the Faithful'.
9.   We shall only mention here the Shi'ite doctrine in its Ja'fari or Twelver varieties (corresponding to the occultation of the twelfth imam),

leaving on one side a number of other doctrinal identities, such as Kharijism, Zaydism, and Isma'ilism.

5
A Survey of Doctrine

1. See Bleuchot, *Droit musulman*, vol. I, pp. 438–66.
2. Quran XXXIII, 59.
3. Quran XXXI, 24.
4. Jacques Berque, *Le Coran: essai de traduction*, Paris: Albin Michel, 1990.
5. The Hanafi authorize a woman who has come of age and is of sound mind to contract a marriage without a guardian. The Shi'a also permit this, if the woman has already been married once.
6. The Shi'a limit compatibility to the capacity of the husband to maintain his wife and to a shared religious belief.
7. Here too there are divergences between schools. For example, the Hanafi accept non-Muslims as witnesses for the marriage of a Muslim with a non-Muslim.
8. Immediate triple repudiation is held to be reprehensible, but it is nevertheless extensively practised. Shi'ite doctrine, along with many modern legal systems, tends to limit exercise of the right of repudiation.
9. We can note the existence of an entire system of guardianship over people who have lost their reason or who are spendthrift. There are also numerous dispositions relating to the status of slaves which, in certain aspects, resemble the rules for guardianship.
10. Hallaq, *Shari'a: Theory, Practice, Transformations*, p. 309.

6
Practices and Institutions of Justice

1. Quran XLII, 15.
2. Quran V, 8.
3. One can thus understand the importance of the question of honour, and that of defilement associated with it, in such a system of collective responsibility. Honour encapsulates the possibility that a person's dignity, because of their status in a group, can be seriously affected – even defiled – by a situation afflicting another person of this same group. Thus, for example, a homicide is perceived as an attack against

the group as a whole. Such an occurrence, regardless of intention, requires reparation.

4. See Émile Tyan, *Histoire de l'organisation judiciaire en pays d'Islam*, Leiden: Brill, 1960; Sami Zubaida, *Law and Power in the Islamic World*, London: I. B. Tauris, 2003.

5. Zubaida, *Law and Power*, p. 41.

6. The story is recounted in Tyan, *Histoire de l'organisation judiciaire* and Zubaida, *Law and Power*.

7. Lawrence Rosen, *The Anthropology of Justice: Law as Culture in Islamic Society*, Cambridge: Cambridge University Press, 1989.

8. Gilles Veinstein, 'L'Empire dans sa grandeur (xvie siècle)', in Robert Mantran (ed.), *Histoire de l'Empire ottoman*, Paris: Fayard, 1989, p. 189.

7
The Invention of Islamic Law

1. See Léon Buskens and Baudouin Dupret, "The Invention of Islamic Law: A History of Western Studies of Islamic Normativity and Their Spread in the Orient", in François Pouillon and Jean-Claude Vatin (eds.), *After Orientalism: Critical Perspectives on Western Agency and Eastern Re-appropriations*, Leiden, Brill, 2015.

8
Sharia in Contemporary Legal Systems

1. See Jan Michiel Otto (ed.), *Sharia Incorporated: A Comparative Overview of the Legal Systems of Twelve Muslim Countries in Past and Present*, Leiden: Leiden University Press, 2010.

2. In Arabic, the word constitution is translated by *dustur*. Numerous political parties describe themselves as 'Constitutionalist', as in Tunisia, where the party in power was called for many years the Neo-Destour.

3. This Code is the most famous work of the jurisconsult 'Abd al-Razzaq al-Sanhuri, and has been the model in most of the Arab countries in the Middle East.

4. See Ardechir Amir-Arjomand, 'La charia en Iran', in Dupret (ed.), *La charia aujourd'hui*.

5. Monia Ben Jemia, 'Le juge tunisien et la légitimation de l'ordre juridique positif par la charia', in Dupret (ed.), *La charia aujourd'hui*, p. 158.

6. Quran II, 275.
7. It is stipulated in the first article that Islam is the religion of the state and that the principles of Sharia are the main source of legislation, while in the second article freedom of conscience is protected and cannot be harmed.

9
The Sharia: Political Uses and Constitutional Renderings

1. See Armando Salvatore, 'La sharia moderne en quête de droit: raison transcendante, métanorme publique et système juridique', *Droit et Société* 39 (1998), pp. 293–316.
2. Dupret, *Au nom de quel droit*.
3. Michel Aflaq, discourse 'À la mémoire du Prophète arabe', 1943, p. 75 (available at http://albaath.online.fr/Francais/COMMEMORATION_DU_PROPHETE_ARABE.htm).
4. Ferrié, 'Usages politiques de la charia'; Baudouin Dupret and Jean-Noël Ferrié, 'Participer au pouvoir c'est imposer la norme: sur l'affaire Abu Zayd (Égypte, 1996–1992)', *Revue française de science politique*, 47, 6 (1997), pp. 762–75.
5. Ferrié, 'Usages politiques de la charia', pp. 88–9.
6. However, some countries such as Indonesia have not done this, while others, such as Turkey, have stressed the secular character of the state.
7. This law, among other things, gave first wives whose husbands secretly contracted another marriage an almost automatic right to divorce.
8. Nathalie Bernard-Maugiron, 'La place de la charia dans la hiérarchie des normes', in Dupret (ed.), *La charia aujourd'hui*, p. 61.
9. Salah Ben Youssef, who was assassinated in 1961, was one of the leaders of the Tunisian national movement. Originally a faithful lieutenant of Bourguiba, he later became his opponent and sworn enemy.
10. Ben Jemia, 'Le juge tunisien et la légitimation de l'ordre juridique positif par la charia'.
11. Mohammed Mouaqit, 'Marginalité de la charia et centralité de la Commanderie des croyants: le cas paradoxal du Maroc', in Dupret (ed.), *La charia aujourd'hui*, p. 150.

10
Sharia in Countries Where Islam is in a Minority

1. See Nathalie Bernard-Maugiron and Baudoin Dupret (eds.), *Ordre public et droit musulman de la famille en Europe et en Afrique du Nord*, Brussels: Bruylant, 2012.

2. See Marie-Claire Foblets, 'Les juges belges et l'application de la loi étrangère en droit de la famille', in Bernard-Maugiron and Dupret (eds.), *Ordre public et droit musulman*.

3. Ibid.

4. See John Bowen, *Shaping British Islam: Sharia Debates and Cultural Repertoires*, Princeton: Princeton University Press, 2013.

5. Louis-Léon Christians, 'Les références belges à l'ordre public comme standard de régulation et révélateur de conflits de valeurs dans le statut des personnes musulmane en dehors du droit international privé', in Bernard-Maugiron and Dupret (eds.), *Ordre public et droit musulman de la famille*.

6. Nadia Marzouki, *L'islam, une religion américaine?* Paris: Seuil, 2013.

7. This typology follows that proposed by Franck Fregosi, 'Usages sociaux de la référence à la charia chez les musulmans d'Europe', in Dupret (ed.), *La charia aujourd'hui*.

8. Hani Ramadan, 'La charia incomprise', *Le Monde*, 9 September 2012.

9. Abdelmadjid Charfi, *L'islam entre le message et l'histoire*, Paris: Albin Michel, 2004, p. 67.

10. Tareq Oubrou, 'La sharî'a de minorité: reflexions pour une intégration légale de l'islam', in Franck Fregosi (ed.), *Lectures contemporaines du droit islamique: Europe-Monde arabe*, Strasbourg: PUS, 2004, p. 000.

11. Oubrou, 'La sharî'ia de minorité', p. 39.

12. Tariq Ramadan, *Les musulmans dans la laïcité: responsabilités et droits des musulmans dans les sociétés occidentales*, Lyons: Tawhid, 1994.

13. Tariq Ramadan, *Mon intime conviction*, Paris: Presses du Châtelet, 2009, p. 86.

14. Maurits Berger, 'Introduction', in M.S. Berger (ed.), *Applying Sharia in the West: Facts, Fears and the Future of Islamic Rules on Family Relations in the West*, Leiden: Leiden University Press, 2013.

15. See Jean-Philippe Bras, 'La controverse autour du mariage de Lille: quel compromis sur la virginité des femmes?' in Mohammed Nachi (ed.), *Les figures du compromis dans les sociétés islamiques: perspectives historiques et socio-anthropologiques*, Paris: Karthala, 2011.

Conclusion

1. Paul Veyne, *Quand notre monde est devenu chrétien*, Paris: Albin Michel, 2007, p. 249.
2. Ibid., p. 263.
3. Marcel Gauchet, *La religion dans la démocratie*, Paris: Gallimard, 1998, p. 29.

Glossary

abrogation (*naskh*): theory of the science of the foundations of doctrine (*'ILM USUL AL-FIQH*) which governs the harmonization of contradictory rules.

apostasy (*ridda*): abandoning one's religion. One of the crimes defined and sanctioned in a set manner by the *HUDUD*.

banditry (*hiraba*): one of the crimes defined and sanctioned in a set manner by the *HUDUD*.

***bay'a*:** the oath of allegiance sworn to political authorities.

***bid'a* (blameworthy innovation):** doctrinal innovation; an invention contrary to orthodox dogma.

blood price (*diya*): principle of financial compensation for a violent crime involving bloodshed.

caliph: the title of the successor to the Prophet in his temporal powers. Sunnis believe that he does not have a successor in religious matters.

Commander of the Faithful (*amir al-mu'minin*): title given to the successor of the Prophet; also given to the Moroccan king.

consumption of wine (*shurb*): one of the acts defined and sanctioned in a set manner according to the *HUDUD*.

doctrinal school (*madhhab*, pl. *madhahib*): regrouping of doctrinal traditions around an eponymous founder; there are four in Sunni Islam: Hanafi, Maliki, Shafi'i, and Hanbali.

doctrine: see *fiqh*.

endowments: see *waqf*.

fasting (*sawm*): the fast of the month of Ramadan is the fourth of the pillars of Islam.

fatwa: doctrinal opinion given by a MUFTI.

fiqh: Islamic doctrine, body of knowledge extracted and derived from SHARIA.

fornication (*zina*): sexual relationships out of wedlock, one of the HUDUD defined and sanctioned in a set manner.

hadith: deeds, acts, and words of the Prophet. An individual tradition belonging to the corpus of the SUNNA.

hajj: the annual pilgrimage to Mecca; the fifth of the five pillars of Islam.

halal: licit, a doctrinal category covering what is authorized.

Hanafi: a doctrinal school of Sunni Islam, named after the scholar Abu Hanifa (699–757).

Hanbali: Sunni doctrinal school, named after the scholar Ibn Hanbal (780–855).

haram: an Arabic adjective describing what is forbidden, the category of the forbidden in the typology of acts.

Hegira (*hijra*): migration of Muhammad to Medina in 621; term used to designate the Islamic calendar.

hisba: principle of justice, based on the Quranic injunction to command good and forbid evil; police responsible for moral affairs and the regulation of markets.

hudud: penalties which are divinely prescribed; their non-observance is sanctioned in a fixed manner by the divine Norm. *Hudud* are also set penalties for certain crimes considered offences against God.

ijma (**consensus**): the consensus of Muslims or of scholars is one of the sources of the science of the foundations of doctrine (*ILM USUL AL-FIQH*).

ijtihad (**effort of interpretation**): a faculty used by a jurisconsult (*MUJTAHID*) to find a solution to a doctrinal problem. One of the techniques of doctrinal reasoning.

'*ilm usul al-fiqh* (**science of the foundations of doctrine**): epistemology and methodology of SHARIA and *FIQH*.

imam: an Arabic word designating the person who stands in front of an assembly, whether to lead prayer or to direct the Muslim community. For the Shi'a, descendants of the Prophet, hereditary leaders endowed with special authority.

istihsan (**preferential reasoning**): one of the forms of doctrinal reasoning which aims to bring to the fore the most suitable solution in the light of the situation, the divine Norm, and the public interest.

jihad: the effort by a believer to follow in the divine path; holy war.

jizya: tax levied on non-Muslim monotheists living in Islamic territory.

jurisconsult (*faqih*, pl. *fuqaha'*): a specialist and practitioner of doctrine (*FIQH*). See also *mufti*; *mujtahid*.

kafir (pl. *kuffar*): polytheist, miscreant.

Kharijites: dissident group within Islam which emerged from the conflict between the caliph 'Ali and the 'Umayyad Mu'awiya, and from the arbitration after the Battle of Siffin (657).

lex talionis: see *qisas*.

mahr: nuptial gift, in the form of money or possessions, paid or promised to a bride by her bridegroom, or by his father. A substantial element of the marriage contract.

Maliki: Sunni doctrinal school, named after the scholar Malik ibn Anas (711–95).

mufti: title given to an expert in giving a doctrinal opinion after consultation; many states have created a post of *mufti* at the head of the administration of religious affairs.

mujtahid: JURISCONSULT exercising *IJTIHAD* (interpretation)

Mu'tazilite: theological school founded on reason and rational thought; flourished under the Abbasid caliphate from the eighth to the eleventh century.

nuptial gift: see *mahr*.

pious foundation: see *waqf*.

positive law: see *qanun*.

prayer: see *salat*.

profession of faith: see *shahada*.

qadi: Arabic word designating an administrator, and by derivation a person invested with the functions of a judge; in Orientalist writings, the Muslim judge.

qanun: an Arabic word of Greek origin, designating the laws promulgated by the temporal power, as opposed to norms of divine inspiration.

qisas (*lex talionis*): retaliatory corporal punishment for an injury, equivalent to that suffered by the victim.

qiyas (**analogy, analogical reasoning**): one of the four sources of Islamic doctrine (*FIQH*); the Arabic term designates a measure of equivalence and, by extension, analogy and reasoning by analogy.

Quran: word of Arabic origin (*qur'an*) which evokes the idea of recitation and designates the text revealed by God.

Quranic exegesis: see *tafsir*.

religious endowments: see *waqf*.

salat (**prayer**): ritual prayer which has to be accomplished at fixed times, five times a day; the second of the pillars of Islam.

Shafi'i: Sunni doctrinal school, derived from the name of the scholar al-Shafi'i (767–820).

shahada: attestation of belief in God and His Prophet; the first of the pillars of Islam.

Sharia: word derived from the Arabic *shari'a*, which means the way that leads to God and designates the divine Norm.

shaykh al-islam: a title granted to the person exercising a ministerial role in the fields of religion and justice; supreme authority in religion in the Ottoman Empire.

Shi'ism (*ahl al-shi'a*): one of the two branches of Islam, with SUNNISM.

shura: consultation, political principle of Quranic origin.

Sunna: Prophetic Tradition, the collected deeds and words of the Prophet and his Companions, which constitute a major source of the divine Norm according to Islamic doctrine.

Sunnism (*ahl al-sunna wa-l-jama'a*): one of the two main doctrinal families of Islam, with SHI'ISM.

tafsir: Quranic exegesis, a literary genre which uses tradition, linguistics, and logic to clarify the meaning of verses.

talaq **(repudiation):** unilateral divorce, a right reserved to husbands.

theft (*sariqa*): one of the crimes with a statutory punishment defined and sanctioned in a set manner by the *HUDUD*.

transactional acts (*mu'amalat*): doctrinal dispositions organizing relations between people.

'ulama **(sing. *'alim*):** scholars, generally of religious sciences.

umma: Arabic word evoking the idea of motherland, designating the community of believers in the world.

untruthful accusation of fornication or adultery (*qadhf*): one of the crimes with a statutory punishment prescribed and sanctioned in a set manner by the *HUDUD*.

usury (*riba*): interest charged on loans, a Quranic notion which is the basis of the forbidding of interest-generating loans.

waqf: inalienable endowment whose income is reserved to a pious foundation.

***wilaya al-faqih* (government by jurisconsults):** doctrine formulated by the Ayatollah Khomeini to justify the establishment of a regime dominated by the Shi'ite clergy.

***zakat* (charity):** the third pillar of Islam.

Index

233